AMERICAN
CAPITAL
and
CANADIAN
RESOURCES

AMERICAN

CAPITAL

and

CANADIAN

RESOURCES

$+$

Hugh G. J. Aitken

1961
Harvard University Press
Cambridge

© Copyright, 1961, by the President and Fellows
of Harvard College

Distributed in Great Britain
by Oxford University Press, London

Library of Congress Catalog Card Number 61–13733

Printed in the United States of America

Preface

The preface to a book, though the first part to be read, is usually the last to be written. As such, it provides the author with an opportunity to excuse the faults of his work, to explain its purpose, and to thank those who helped him along the way. This book probably still has many faults, but I have tried to eliminate those that were apparent to me. As for its purpose, if this is not made clear in the first chapter I have no confidence in my ability to make it clear within the few pages of a preface. There remains, therefore, only the third function that a preface can perform: that of acknowledging assistance and recording gratitude. This is, in the present instance, not only a duty but also a most welcome opportunity.

Three institutions granted me hospitality and the use of their facilities while this book was in preparation, and to each of them I owe a considerable debt. During the summer of 1958, I enjoyed the privilege of working at the Duke University Commonwealth-Studies Center as a member of the summer seminar on Canadian-American economic relations. For the academic year 1958–59 I held a National Research Professorship, granted by the Brookings Institution, which made it possible for me to exploit the excellent research facilities available in Washington, to renew a number of old friendships in Canada, and to acquire new ones. During the year 1959–60 I had the honor of holding the Skelton-Clark Fellowship at Queen's University in Kingston, Ontario, an appointment which provided an invaluable opportunity to exchange ideas with Canadian scholars and, in an atmosphere free from the normal distractions of university life, to reduce these ideas to writing. I must also express my appreciation of the liberality shown by the University of California, which granted me the unusual privilege of a two years' leave of absence, and of the generous tolerance of my colleagues on the Riverside campus of the university who, because of my absence, were called upon to carry a heavier burden of teaching and administrative duties than would normally have fallen to their lot.

A number of individuals gave me help, guidance, and encouragement during the writing of this book, and to them I am most grateful. Professor Frank A. Knox and Professor John J. Deutsch of Queen's University were good enough to read and criticize an early draft of the manuscript; the final version has benefited considerably from their advice. Mrs. Penelope Hartland Thunberg, of Washington, D.C., not only read Chapter II in an earlier version and gave me the benefit of her criticism but also graciously permitted the use of her estimates of the Canadian balance of payments before 1900, prepared at the National Bureau of Economic Research, before they were published. Mr. Samuel Pizer of the United States Department of Commerce and Mr. E. B. Carty of the Dominion Bureau of Statistics were generous with their advice and suggestions.

None of these individuals, of course, is to be held responsible for any errors of omission or commission that may be present in the final version.

The short passage from the pen of Mr. Bruce Hutchison, quoted on page 112, is produced by kind permission of the editors of *The Financial Post.*

Lastly, I would like to record the debt that I owe to my wife, not only for her help in criticizing the manuscript and preparing it for the press, but also for the support and sympathy that she unfailingly provided during those moments of discouragement that all writers must accept as part of the hazards of their profession.

H.G.J.A.

Riverside, California
July 1961

Contents

Tables

Tables

APPENDIX

Charts

AMERICAN
CAPITAL
and
CANADIAN
RESOURCES

CHAPTER I

Regional Integration and
Economic Development

International economic relations since the end of World War II have been characterized by two conflicting tendencies: On the one hand, persistent attempts have been made to reconstruct a relatively unfettered system of multilateral trade and payments similar to that which flourished during the late nineteenth century. On the other, there has been a tendency toward regional groupings, regional associations, and regional agreements.

Essential instruments in the implementation of the first line of policy have been the General Agreement on Tariffs and Trade, the American Reciprocal Trade Agreements Act, and the two new international agencies established in the postwar years: the International Monetary Fund and the International Bank for Reconstruction and Development. Emphasis has been laid on the reduction of tariffs on a multilateral, nondiscriminatory basis, the extension of tariff concessions through the most-favored-nation principle,[1] the elimination of quotas except in special circumstances, and the avoidance of competitive currency devaluation. The primary objective has been the elimination of nationalism in trade policy.

Though overshadowed at first by the popularity and achievements of international policies, the regional approach has become more evident in recent years and appears to be growing in strength. It reflects an awareness of the benefits — economic, political, and strategic — that national states may achieve by making limited concessions of sovereignty to a central authority, by forming associations of limited membership, and by integrating their policies in limited fields. It has come to be interpreted, particularly by the middle powers, as presenting a third alternative for national policy, a compromise between outright nationalism and complete internationalism, avoiding the economic and strategic hazards of the first and the practical limitations of the second.[2]

In the immediate postwar period, regional integration was directed toward the specific goals of defense and economic reconstruction. Conspicuous examples in the military sphere were the North Atlantic Treaty Organization, the South East Asia Treaty Organization, and the ANZUS defense pact. In the field of regional economic integration, the Organization for European Economic Cooperation was of prime importance. More limited in their purposes, but reflecting strictly European needs more closely, were the European Payments Union, the European Coal and Steel Community, and the European Atomic Energy Community. One example of complete economic integration appeared early: the Benelux union, including Belgium, the Netherlands, and Luxemburg.

Out of these limited measures of regional integration there has developed more recently a tendency toward regional integration on a broader scale and for more general objectives. This has been carried farthest in the case of the so-called European Common Market — more correctly, the European Economic Community, a grouping of six nations (France, West Germany, Italy, Belgium, Luxemburg, and the Netherlands) which have agreed to eliminate, over a period of twelve to fifteen years, all tariffs and quotas on the movement of industrial products among themselves, to establish a common tariff against the rest of the world, to harmonize their labor and welfare policies, and to permit capital and labor to move freely within the area. At the end of the transition period, these nations will in effect form a single economy, a compact geographical and industrial unit with a market of more than 165 million persons.

Also in process of formation is the European Free Trade Association, a group of seven nations (the United Kingdom, Norway, Sweden, Denmark, Austria, Switzerland, and Portugal) scattered around the perimeter of the Common Market which, while recognizing the advantages of some degree of economic integration, are unwilling to commit themselves to the degree of political integration envisaged by the EEC. In particular, the members of the Free Trade Area intend to maintain their separate national tariffs against the outside world, though eliminating tariffs among themselves; member countries will be free to follow reasonably independent commercial policies; and there is no intention of coordinating working conditions and social welfare programs or of allowing unlimited freedom of movement for labor and capital.

Measures have also been taken in other parts of the world looking toward economic integration on a regional basis. By the Treaty of Montevideo, signed on February 18, 1960, seven Latin American nations (Argentina, Brazil, Chile, Mexico, Uruguay, Paraguay, and Peru) with a combined population of approximately 200 million people, agreed to set up a free trade area by the gradual elimination of tariffs and other restrictions on most of their mutual trade over a twelve-year period. Three other nations — El Salvador, Guatemala, and Honduras — signed an agreement in early February, 1960, designed to bring into existence in five years a common market with complete internal free trade and an equalized tariff against other countries; Costa Rica and Nicaragua were at one time expected to become members of this common market, but political difficulties have excluded them for the time being. Meanwhile, all twenty Latin American nations are involved in negotiations looking toward the conversion of the whole continent into a free trade zone, and serious proposals are appearing for the adoption of similar policies in other parts of the world.

What success will attend these experiments, what policies will accompany them, and what implications they will have for the world economy are at present matters of opinion only. Already, however, it seems clear that, whatever type of world economy will finally emerge, it will not be a world economy reconstructed on the nineteenth-century model. It will not be, that is to say, an economy of which the units are nation states and their associated colonies. Rather, it will be one composed of regional groupings — sets of countries which retain most of the formal features of national sovereignty but which have accepted varying degrees of economic, political, and military integration with each other.

Observers who are committed, emotionally or intellectually, to the more universalistic approach see in these emerging regional systems a threat to the principles and practices of international economic relations that have been painfully evolved in the postwar years. Sometimes, too, regional integration is interpreted as presaging the breakup of the western alliance, a reversion to protectionism, and the division of the noncommunist world into a series of competitive and mutually hostile trading systems. It is idle to pretend that such consequences are not possible. Yet the tendency toward regional integration can be interpreted in more positive and hopeful terms. Much depends on the particular policies adopted, but it can hardly be denied that the potential benefits of integration are very large. Nor are these potential benefits exclusively economic; the political implications are of no less significance. In the case of the European Economic Community, but not of the Free Trade Area, one of the major arguments for economic integration is that it will pave the way for eventual political integration. What form such political integration may take it is impossible to say; its organizational form is in any event of less significance than the fact that the nations concerned are apparently prepared to accept, and indeed to welcome, a sacrifice of individual national sovereignty. To a large extent, indeed, this sacrifice has already been made: countries that have agreed to eliminate tariffs and quotas, to bring their internal economic and social policies into uniformity, and to permit free mobility of capital and labor have already made substantial cessions of sovereignty. And if to this large measure of economic integration there is added a pooling of military resources, the area in which the member nations can be said to exercise independent sovereignty must shrink very substantially.

We do not yet know whether any or all of the regional economic systems now contemplated or in existence will prove viable. Nor can we predict with any confidence whether their policies will tend toward restrictionism and self-sufficiency or alternatively provide a new and firmer basis for freedom of trade and investment. Some of the issues raised by the tendency toward regional integration are, however, already clear. In the first place, regional economic integration in one area tends to promote regional economic integration in others. Since it is intrinsically discriminatory between internal and external suppliers, integration tends to stimulate competitive integration as a means of retaliation, of equalizing bargaining power, and of developing outlets for trade diverted from its original markets. Secondly, regional economic integration tends to broaden into political and military integration, partly because of the necessity for harmonizing domestic economic and social policies and partly because the strategic security of the regional system becomes one and indivisible. And lastly, the feasibility and attractiveness of regional integration depend upon the degree of insecurity and the danger of military attack. Extreme insecurity encourages military and economic affiliation with one or other of the major powers in a system of satellitic or client states. Regional integration may appear as a process of partial disengagement from such a system; but it may also develop as a means of reinforcing the alliance in the face of disintegrative tendencies.

In North America, regional integration has developed along lines different from those characteristic of the emerging regional systems in Europe. There have been as yet no serious proposals for a customs union or a free trade area; reciprocal abolition of tariffs between Canada and the United States was last suggested in 1911, when it was rejected by Canada. The political unification of the two nations is at present out of the question; neither country desires it and both would have great difficulty in adjusting to it. At first glance, indeed, it might appear that there is little in common between the economic structure that has emerged in North America and the regional systems that are emerging in Europe. Regional integration, however, is not always the product of treaties and deliberate government policies; it can emerge more imperceptibly, as the by-product of private trade and investment decisions, of complementary resource structures, and of geographical proximity. Canada and the United States are in fact the leading contemporary example of regional economic integration. The process of integration has already gone very far and, if present trends continue, will go farther. What is emerging in North America is continental economic integration on a massive scale.[3]

The extent to which the Canadian and American economies are already integrated with each other is evident from the grossest measures. Since Canada became a nation in 1867, the value of Canadian-American trade has increased some eighty-fold; during the same period, total world trade has increased only about twenty times. The proportion of Canadian imports originating in the United States, which was approximately one-third in 1870 and two-thirds in 1914, has exceeded 70 per cent in recent years. Canada sold about one-half of its exports in the United States in 1870 and a little over one-third before World War I; since World War II, the proportion has been approximately 60 per cent.[4] Of total United States merchandise exports in 1958, 21.6 per cent were sold in Canada; in the same year Canada accounted for 28 per cent of United States imports for consumption.[5] Of all the nations with which the United States carries on trade, Canada is the most important by a substantial margin, both as a customer and as a source of supply. Equally suggestive of the closeness of integration are the investment statistics: of all private long-term foreign investments of the United States, nearly 40 per cent have been placed in Canada, more than in the whole of Europe or the whole of Latin America.[6] Total nonresident investment in Canada at the end of 1958 was estimated at $19.1 billion; of this more than 75 per cent represented United States investment.[7] Canada in recent years has been importing capital at a rate of over $1 billion annually, relying on foreign resources to finance more than a third of her net capital formation; of this capital inflow more than 80 per cent has come from the United States.[8]

Statistics such as these illustrate how close the economic relationships between Canada and the United States have already become. But there are other sorts of evidence: the correspondence between the two countries in business organization and practices, consumer tastes, and advertising techniques; the intimate linkages between many of the largest corporations in Canada and parent corporations in the United States; the dominance of certain Canadian industries by American-owned and American-controlled firms; Canada's substantial dependence on American technology and American entrepreneurship, particularly in the resource industries; the complex networks of railroads, highways, inland waterways, pipelines, and electric transmission lines that integrate the whole continent in a single transportation system; and the extreme sensitivity of the smaller country — smaller in population and wealth, but not in area — to the policies of the larger. Economic integration is far from complete; indeed it may never be complete, for any proposal to carry the process through to its logical conclusion (logical, that is, in economic terms) would encounter significant resistance in both countries. Nevertheless, the economic obstacles to complete integration are probably less in North America than they are in Europe. Free mobility of capital and labor in both directions across the border, proximity, similarity of language and culture, and a substantial degree of complementarity in resources and needs have already produced an approximation to a single continental economic system. If the only relevant factor were the economic adjustments involved, completion of the process would be relatively easy.

In recent years, the economic pressures toward continental integration have been strongly reinforced by pressures arising from the requirements of security and continental defense. Advances in the technology of warfare have for the first time exposed the heartland of continental North America to the possibility of crippling attack. At the same time, they have increased the complexity and cost of defense to a level that no single nation with a relatively small population and limited industrial capacity can support unaided. Canada therefore has had no feasible alternative but to integrate her defense arrangements as closely as possible with those of the United States. This has implied active support of the NATO alliance, cooperation with the United States in the construction of radar warning systems, complete integration of air defenses in the NORAD organization, and dependence on American research and production facilities for defensive missiles. The United States, for its part, has found cooperation with Canada essential for the defense of the Arctic frontier. To all intents and purposes, the strategic defense of the continent is already completely integrated.

The implications of strategic security have also been evident in the economic sphere. Canadian natural resources would, even under the most secure conditions, be a prime source of supply for American industry. The uncertainties of the cold war and the risks involved in dependence on foreign sources of supply that may be cut off either by military attack or by intransigent nationalism have in recent years placed a premium on the development of resources in Canada, a nation closely allied to the United States in ideology, hospitable in its attitude to foreign investment, and inextricably involved in the same defense system. The results have been evident in an unprecedented volume of American investment in the Canadian resource industries — iron ore, oil, gas, tungsten, uranium for a limited period, and many others. In addition to these strategic considerations there has been rising concern in the United States over the increasing depletion of certain domestic sources of raw materials and the unavailability of others — a concern that was expressed most positively in the Paley Report of 1952.[9] Anxiety over the trend toward dependence on imports of industrial raw materials and the obvious security risks associated with resource development in other areas have given Canadian sources of supply a unique significance for the United States.

Defense and development have combined in the postwar years to reinforce tendencies toward continental integration whose origins can be traced far back into the nineteenth century. Economically, the ties between the two countries are close and are becoming closer. In defense matters, their policies and resources are virtually completely integrated. Politically, however, Canada and the United States remain separate and independent sovereign states. No cessions of sovereignty have been made.

Both nations are jealous of their independence: Canada would resist political absorption by the United States no less vigorously than the United States would resist political absorption by Canada. No common market has been seriously proposed; no free trade area is at present under consideration. Regional economic integration has emerged, not for political reasons and not by a deliberately engineered elimination of trade barriers, but as the net result of the drive for economic development on both sides of the border, of the free mobility of capital, labor, and enterprise, and of the complementarity of resources and markets. The probability is that the process will continue in the future along the same lines as in the past, unless indeed some external threat leads both nations to seek means to accelerate it.

Bilateral tariff reductions between Canada and the United States, perhaps leading eventually to the formation of a North American free trade area, would certainly accelerate the process of continental integration and bring substantial economic benefits to both countries. It would be idle to pretend that such an outcome is not possible in view of the tendencies toward regional integration in other parts of the world. Both Canada and the United States have supported integration in Europe, though they would prefer one regional system to two; both, however, face the possibility of serious damage to their external trade should the policies of the European systems turn decisively toward discrimination. The close economic relations that already exist between the two countries, the substantial measure of economic integration that mobility of capital and labor has already produced, their commitment to a common defense system, and their similarity in social structure and values would make the mechanics of complete integration relatively simple. This is not to say, however, that complete economic integration is probable. On the contrary, if such a move were ever proposed, resistance would be serious, particularly in Canada.

Complete economic integration with the United States would be resisted in Canada for very much the same reasons that have led certain nations in Europe to resist integration in the European Economic Community. Of fundamental importance is the conviction that economic integration threatens the survival of the nation state as a separate identity. In Europe, this has been a powerful deterrent to economic integration. In Canada, where the sense of national identity is of much more recent origin than in Europe, where in consequence the preservation of national identity is regarded as a matter of major importance, and where complete economic integration would in effect mean absorption by a single dominant neighbor, it is a consideration sufficiently potent to make an objective appraisal of the benefits and costs of integration very difficult.

Resistance by Canada to economic integration with the United States, even in the relatively gradual and limited form in which integration has so far appeared, has shown itself recently in a resurgence of anti-American sentiment and a growing sensitivity to any aspects of American policy that seem, or can be made to seem, contrary to Canadian national interests. Concern over relations with the United States is, of course, no new phenomenon in Canadian public life; over the past century, it has been a major issue in Canadian politics at least once in every decade.[10] In the intensity with which the issues have been debated, however, the postwar years can challenge comparison with any previous period in Canada's history. There has been a general, if sometimes grudging, recognition of the economic benefits that have accrued to Canada from the inflow of American capital and entrepreneurship; access to the American market for raw materials is correctly interpreted as the keystone of Canada's current prosperity; the large-scale resource development projects that have been undertaken in response to American needs are regarded with pride as major contributions to the nation's economic strength; and the proved wealth of Canada's natural resources is taken as justifying optimistic forecasts of the country's economic future. The dominant theme has been one of satisfaction, of increasing confidence, of pride in Canada's growing stature as a nation. Yet, accompanying this theme and interacting with it in persistent counterpoint, there has been serious concern over the implications for Canada of its increasingly intimate relations with its continental partner. There have been a multiplicity of minor frictions and annoyances, the staple raw material for innumerable Canadian editorials; there have been in some cases major conflicts of interest; the difficulties that are inevitable when two nations are linked together by such intimate ties have been exacerbated by Canada's distrust of her partner's motives, by a history of resistance to American continental imperialism, and by a chronic insensitivity on the part of the United States. Above all, there has been in Canada a profound but seldom explicitly stated concern over the long-run costs of economic integration — costs that are reckoned not by the economic calculus but rather in terms of national pride and a sense of national identity that is valued all the more highly because it has been achieved so recently.

These reactions have been accentuated by the disparity in size and bargaining power of the two participants, by American indifference to Canadian sentiment, and by an uncomfortable recognition in Canada that the process of integration has already gone so far that it may be irreversible, or reversible only at considerable cost to Canada. In addition, there has been a reluctance in both countries to face up to the implications of integration. Inconsistency in policy has contributed its quota to misunderstanding and resentment.

Few people in the United States are aware how far economic integration with Canada has already proceeded. Fewer still have given any thought to the implications of economic integration for national policy. If Canada is now, as some have alleged, an economic satellite of the United States, it is a satellite acquired almost by inadvertence, as an incident in the rise of the United States to industrial and military supremacy. This does not mean, however, that the Canadian reaction to American dominance can be ignored. More is at stake here than merely relations with Canada. If the United States is to retain the leadership of the noncommunist world, it must accept as relevant to its interests the attitudes and opinions of those nations that it presumes to lead. Hostile sentiment cannot be ignored merely because it has not yet affected official government policies. It may be that Canada's ability to retaliate when injured by the United States is limited; it may be that, as long as Canada regards rapid economic development as a major goal of policy, there are few alternatives but to accept dependence on American capital and American markets. But if in the case of Canada, a country closely allied in ideology and values, where economic integration has taken place almost wholly by nongovernmental action, the accompaniment of integration is continuous resentment and growing hostility, one may reasonably feel uneasiness about the probable reaction in other parts of the world.

Canada, to be sure, is not Cuba. The reactions that in
the one area show themselves in revolution and violence
are in the other merely a disquieting undercurrent to relations basically friendly. Yet the two cases have enough
in common to suggest that economic integration with
the United States, even when clearly in the economic interests of the nation involved, carries with it no built-in
guarantee of political and social acceptability. In North
America, as in Europe, economic integration can appear
a liberating process or a confining one. If economic integration with the United States implies vulnerability to
American policies decided upon purely for reasons of
domestic political advantage in the United States, it will
be resisted or, if it cannot be resisted, it will be accompanied by hostility and resentment. It is not to be expected that other nations will willingly accept dependence
on American capital and American markets if the price
is submission to American nationalism.

In the case of Canada, the issues posed by economic
integration with the United States have become very
clear. Canada as a nation has survived only by virtue
of its resistance to American expansionism. This is the
one constant theme of Canadian history: the nation exists because it has consistently refused to accept absorption by the United States. Yet at the present day every
prospect for further economic development open to
Canada appears to carry with it, as an inescapable consequence, increasing integration in a continental economy
in which the United States must be the dominant partner.
The conflict is stark. On the one hand acceptance of the
integrative tendencies promises great economic benefit;
involvement with the United States is in many respects
inescapable; the feasibility of resistance is doubtful; and
alternative policies are either not available or extremely

costly. On the other hand, resistance to absorption by
the United States is the very core of Canadian nationalism; traditional ties with Europe and the Commonwealth
are still strong; despite extreme exposure to American
values, there is a developing sense of national identity
which further integration with the United States seems
certain to submerge; and, underlying all other sources of
resistance, there is a conviction that Canada may have
its own distinctive contribution to make to human history,
and a profound reluctance to see this possibility eliminated. Every economic inducement, every opportunity
for economic development impels Canada to accede to
the continental pressures that now impinge on her. Every
memory of historical tradition, every hope for the future
preservation of national identity impels her to resist
them.

From one point of view, this is a distinctively Canadian
problem, for no other nation finds itself confronted with
quite such limited alternatives as Canada does. Regarded
in a different light, however, the problem is much more
general, for it involves the ability of smaller nations to
survive as separate entities in a world which increasingly
makes the formation of larger units almost essential.
Largely because of the uncertainty and insecurity that
have characterized international relations in the postwar
period, pressures for integration — either in a system of
alliances based on one of the major powers or in some
more limited regional system — have become intense.
To the extent that this tendency serves to promote stability and security, it is to be welcomed. To the extent that
it involves the submergence of national differences and
the domination of smaller nations by larger ones, its
virtues are more questionable. The issue that is raised is
a fundamental one. To what extent is it possible to attain

the positive benefits of regional integration — in terms of economic development and greater security — while at the same time preserving what is valuable and constructive in the traditions of individual nations? Is it possible for a nation to accept economic and military integration with a richer and more powerful neighbor without sacrificing its political independence and its hopes for fostering a distinctive national culture? There is no net gain in the submergence of nationalism in the smaller nations if it is accompanied by an increase in the already swollen nationalism of the larger ones. For Canada, in particular, a form of integration that represented merely absorption and left no room for the survival of a distinctive national tradition would have little to commend it.

What then are the alternatives open to Canada? The beginning of wisdom, in dealing with problems of this kind, is an appreciation of the limits within which choices must be made. And this in turn requires above all an understanding of the long-run historical trends that have created the present situation and, if they continue, will shape the future. With this in mind, we shall turn first of all to a historical examination of the movements of capital between the United States and Canada, since it is in these capital transfers that we find reflected most clearly the forces that have tended to integrate the two countries in a single economic system. Next, we shall analyze how the pattern of development in the Canadian economy has come to be determined by the economic opportunities presented by continental integration, and in particular how American capital and the American market have stimulated in Canada the growth of a series of resource industries that we call the new staples. This will be followed by an analysis of the Canadian reaction to the pressures that are bringing a continental economy into existence; here our attention will be focused not on the particular day-to-day causes of friction, for these are things of the moment only, but rather on the more fundamental attitudes and values that determine how Canadians interpret the situation in which they now find themselves. And finally we shall take up the implications of our analysis for national policy, in the United States and in Canada, expressing these not as prescriptions but rather as alternative possible choices, differing in their feasibility, which each country may make and which will affect their future relations differently.

CHAPTER II

American Capital in Canada:
The Statistical Evidence

A fully adequate explanation of how Canada and the United States have come to form something approaching a single economic system would require the writing of an economic history of North America. No such ambitious task will be attempted here. Our present interest is in only one of the processes that have contributed to this situation: the investment in Canada of United States capital. Only one of the processes, but one that can reasonably be called fundamental, for the relatively unrestricted mobility of capital between Canada and the United States has done more to integrate the economies of the two countries than any other single factor except geography.

The word "capital" has been defined in a variety of ways, some of them bordering on the metaphysical. For our purposes, it is sufficient to say that when we speak of a transfer of capital from the United States to Canada, we refer to a situation in which residents of the United States acquire assets in Canada (or reduce their liabilities there). Transactions of this sort can occur in a number of ways: A resident of the United States may, for example, purchase securities in a Canadian corporation or the bonds of a Canadian government; or he may export goods to Canada and leave the proceeds on deposit in that country; or, if he owns a business in Canada, he may "plow back" the profits of that business instead of withdrawing them as dividends. What these various transactions have in common is the fact that some person (an individual or a corporation) resident in the United States acquires ownership rights to property in Canada.

Most but not all transactions of this sort appear in the balance-of-payments statistics of the countries involved. The balance of payments is a kind of large-scale statement of a country's accounts with the rest of the world; it includes all public and private international transactions in which that country is involved. Conventionally, it has two parts: the current account and the capital account. The current account includes payments and receipts for the import and export of commodities; transportation and other commercial services; immigrants' remittances and the expenditures of tourists; and interest and dividends due to nonresidents. Receipts (or, more precisely, claims to payment) are conventionally given a positive sign, and payments (counterclaims) a negative one. Receipts and payments on current account may exactly cancel out or, as happens more frequently, show a negative or positive net balance.

The capital account items relate to changes in a

country's external assets and liabilities. They include the sale of new securities abroad; redemptions, loans, and repayments; receipts and payments from the purchase and sale of outstanding securities; branch plant capital transactions; and changes in monetary gold and externally held cash balances. An addition to external assets is conventionally given a negative sign and an addition to liabilities a positive one. The capital account, taken as a whole, may be in exact balance — a rather unlikely possibility — or show an excess of positive or negative items. If the net balance on capital account is positive, the country is accumulating more liabilities abroad than it is accumulating assets; that is to say, it is borrowing abroad on balance or "importing capital."

The current account balance and the capital account balance must be equal but of opposite sign. For if a country is paying out on current account more than it is taking in, this can only mean that it is getting into debt to other countries, or in other words that it is accumulating liabilities abroad. A deficit on current account must therefore be offset by a surplus on capital account, and vice versa. The fact that the current account and capital account balances must exactly offset each other is, of course, purely a matter of definition. For the economic historian, however, this accounting identity has the fortunate result that it provides him with two alternative methods of estimating how much a country was borrowing or lending abroad in any given period. There is, first of all, what we may call the direct method. This involves identifying and adding up all the positive and negative transactions in the capital account, arriving finally at an estimate of total net capital imports or exports. Alternatively, there is the indirect method, by which we work with the items that make up the current account, adding up all the receipts and payments on current account, and identifying the sum (negative or positive as the case may be) with net capital imports or exports.

If this were a perfect world, the two methods would yield identical results. More often, the results are slightly different because of the difficulty of enumerating completely all the various types of transactions. In official balance-of-payments statistics for recent years, the net movement of capital and the current account balance are always exactly equal, any difference between the two sets of results being taken care of by the insertion of a small item (called the residual or balancing item) which is tucked discreetly in at the foot of the table to represent "unrecorded capital movements and errors and omissions." For earlier periods of history, the discrepancies are sometimes quite large, despite the most conscientious efforts to eliminate them.

If we are interested solely in the total amount of capital that a country exported or imported on balance in a given period, the net balance on current account is a perfectly adequate measure. It is, however, a global figure and, in the absence of other information, it is not possible to say, for example, exactly from which other countries the capital was borrowed or to which it was lent, or what forms the transfer of capital took, or which sectors of the economy were affected by it, or the extent to which the net movement represented a partial offsetting of inflows and outflows. Even if the balance of payments on current account is available on a country-by-country basis the geographical origin of a country's capital imports cannot be determined without ambiguity because of the possibility of multilateral transactions; a loan floated by Canada in London, for example, may be used to finance imports from the United States. To answer questions such as these, there is no substitute for a direct estimate based on an actual count of capital transactions.

If direct estimates are available, they can be broken down in various ways. The area of origin of a country's capital imports is always of interest, particularly if shifts from one source of borrowing to another can be discerned. Similarly, we may ask which sectors of a country's economy were attracting capital imports, since this throws light on the motives of the foreign investors and on the pattern of growth of the domestic economy. Beyond this, two basic distinctions between different types of capital movements must be noted: that between long- and short-term transactions and that between portfolio and direct investment.

The distinction between long- and short-term capital movements is one of those issues that seem simple and clear-cut but in fact are quite the opposite. Conventionally, if the capital is lent for less than one year (some authorities say three or even five years), it is said to be a short-term capital movement; if for longer than this, it is described as long-term. Examples of the first type would be open-book commercial credits, bank deposits held abroad, and bills of exchange; typical of the second would be bonds, corporate shares, and mortgages. For the statistician, this is simple and convenient. The theoretical and historical difficulty arises from the fact that the form of the commercial instrument used is not an entirely reliable guide. Nominally long-term investments, such as corporate securities, may in fact be held for short periods if there is a ready market on which they can be traded. Some writers, therefore, make the distinction in terms of the motives of the investor: If the capital is transferred

with the expectation that it will be repatriated within a
year, it should be defined as a short-term movement, no
matter what form the loan operation takes.

In the pages that follow, we shall be concerned primarily with long-term capital, and perhaps it will be
sufficient if, ignoring many difficulties of definition, we
define this as capital invested in the expectation that the
investment will not be liquidated in the near future and
that it will earn income over an appreciable period.[1] It
should be borne in mind, however, that statistics of a
country's capital imports, unless the contrary is clearly
stated, include short- as well as long-term capital movements.

The distinction between direct and portfolio investment appears to present fewer complexities. Essentially,
the criterion is whether or not the investment carries with
it control over the enterprise in which the investment is
made. Direct investments are those in which control lies
with the foreign investor: The clearest example is the
establishment of a branch plant in Canada by a United
States corporation that retains complete ownership. Portfolio investments, on the other hand, are typically scattered minority holdings of stocks and bonds which do
not carry with them control: All foreign holdings of
Canadian government bonds, for example, are clearly
portfolio investments.[2]

This seems clear enough until we raise the awkward
question, "What constitutes control?" Difficult issues are
involved here. Statistically, the problem is solved by
using as the criterion of control the percentage of common stock owned. The Canadian Dominion Bureau of
Statistics, for example, classifies as direct investments all
concerns in Canada which are known to have 50 per
cent or more of their voting stock held in one country

outside Canada; plus a few concerns where it is known from other evidence that effective control is held by a parent concern even though it owns less than 50 per cent of the stock; plus a small number of Canadian companies which have no parent concerns but of which more than 50 per cent of the stock is owned in a single foreign country and where control is believed to rest with nonresidents.[3] This is not a tidy definition; at best it is purely formal. Control in this sense is consistent with considerable autonomy in management. It is by no means uncommon, for example, to find a Canadian subsidiary of a United States corporation urging the Canadian government to secure a modification in the United States tariff while its parent corporation urges the United States government to refuse it.

One further complexity remains to be faced. There are certain changes in a country's international investment position which are not reflected in the capital account of the balance of payments. The most important of these arise from the reinvestment of earnings by foreign-owned enterprises. In a sense, these are domestic transactions. Nevertheless, they have a significant influence on foreign indebtedness. One consequence of this is that it is an unsatisfactory procedure — though it may be the best possible one — to sum up, over a period of years, the net capital inflows into a country, as shown by the balance of payments, and to equate this total with the net increase in that country's foreign indebtedness over the period. If there has been reinvestment of earnings by foreign-owned enterprises in the meantime, this procedure will seriously underestimate the growth in foreign indebtedness. Changes in the valuation of assets and the effects of international migration and inheritances where no cash remittances are involved also introduce complexities.[4] To avoid this difficulty, estimates of a country's foreign indebtedness are usually made (when the available information permits it) by taking an inventory of the value of foreign investments in that country at certain dates. Serious problems of valuation arise in this connection, but these are discussed in easily accessible sources and need not be mentioned here.[5]

Bearing in mind these basic definitions and the problems they involve, we can now begin our survey of foreign investment in Canada. First, as to historical coverage: The official estimates published by the Canadian Dominion Bureau of Statistics go no farther back in time than 1926; to the historian, this is only yesterday. The United States Department of Commerce has made available annual estimates of the aggregate outflow of capital from that country from 1919 to the present, together with scattered figures for earlier periods, but a continuous series for the net outflow to Canada begins only in 1946. For periods earlier than 1926, we are dependent on the work of private investigators who, lacking the aid of a permanent staff and reporting organization, had to make the best use they could of information collected for other purposes, piecing together what data they could find and estimating the totals as closely as honesty and a professional conscience would permit.

The most courageous attempt to extend our knowledge of Canada's capital imports back in time has been made by Professor Clare Pentland of the University of Manitoba.[6] Working mostly from commodity trade figures, supplemented by information on loans placed in other countries and expenditures in Canada for British military establishments, Pentland offers the following estimates of Canadian imports of capital on private and public account in the middle decades of the nineteenth century (Table 1).

TABLE 1

Imports of Capital into Canada, Totals by Periods, 1827–75

Period	Excluding military expenditures ($ millions)	Including military expenditures ($ millions)
1827–37	10	25
1841–49	15	35
1850–59	100	100
1860–67	46	46
1868–75	200	200

Source. H. C. Pentland, "Further Observations," pp. 403–410.

If we leave out of account the money spent in the Canadian provinces for the maintenance of British forces, most of the rest of the capital imported in this period was expended on transportation improvements. Canal construction accounts for almost the whole of the $25 million acquired on nonmilitary account in the first two periods (1827–49). The jump to $100 million in the period 1850–59 reflects borrowings on public and private account for railroad construction, as does the figure of $200 million for the period 1868–75; economic difficulties and a retardation of railroad construction in the intervening years explain the decline to $46 million. The source of the borrowings was Great Britain; if there was any lending on balance from the United States, it is too insignificant to show in the statistics. The initiative in securing the loans was in general taken by the Canadian provincial governments.

Quantities are significant only in comparison with other quantities. However indispensable these imports of capital were for the economy of the Canadian provinces in this period, they were relatively small compared to the quantities of capital being exported from Britain (and, to a lesser extent, from France and Germany) to other parts of the world in the same period. In the first half of the century, British capital exports went principally to Europe and to the United States. The governments of the American states alone had absorbed nearly $170 million of British capital by 1839.[7] It was not until the second half of the century, and particularly the years after 1875, that the interest of British investors turned in any substantial way to such then "underdeveloped" areas as South America, Africa, Australia, and Canada. Private capital in the nineteenth century moved internationally in response to profit expectations, and the plain fact of the matter was that, through most of the nineteenth century, the profit opportunities that the Canadian provinces could offer were not, in a relative sense, very attractive.

Our knowledge of the flow of capital into Canada in the latter part of the century rests largely on the calculations made by Penelope Hartland, whose estimates of the balance on current account (in the form of five-year moving averages) are summarized in Table 2. This indirect calculation yields a total net capital inflow of $957 million for the period 1868–99. Canadian capital invested abroad over the same period is estimated at $109 million, so that the gross inflow of foreign capital was $1,066 million.[8]

Direct calculations of the inflow of capital in this period are made particularly hazardous by the difficulty of estimating United States direct investment. Hartland estimates that at the time of Confederation in 1867, the total amount of outside capital invested in Canada was

TABLE 2

Canada: Summary Balance of Payments on Current Account, 1868-99
(millions of dollars)

Period	Commodity exports	Commodity imports	Balance on commodity account	Balance on other current items	Net balance on current account
1868-72	72.9	-89.6	-16.7	0.2	-16.5
1869-73	79.0	-100.8	-21.8	0.1	-21.7
1870-74	82.3	-111.3	-29.0	-0.8	-29.8
1871-75	83.4	-115.9	-32.5	-1.8	-34.3
1872-76	83.5	-114.4	-30.9	-3.3	-34.2
1873-77	81.7	-109.8	-28.1	-3.9	-32.0
1874-78	78.9	-101.8	-22.9	-6.1	-29.0
1875-79	78.1	-93.6	-15.5	-7.2	-22.7
1876-80	80.8	-91.2	-10.4	-7.8	-18.2
1877-81	85.2	-94.4	-9.2	-8.3	-17.5
1878-82	89.7	-100.1	-10.4	-9.2	-19.6
1879-83	93.6	-107.3	-13.7	-9.7	-23.4
1880-84	95.7	-112.8	-17.1	-11.3	-28.4
1881-85	94.5	-114.9	-20.4	-13.3	-33.7
1882-86	92.0	-114.1	-22.1	-15.8	-37.9
1883-87	89.9	-111.3	-21.4	-18.0	-39.4
1884-88	88.9	-109.0	-20.1	-19.9	-40.0
1885-89	89.3	-110.2	-20.9	-21.7	-42.6
1886-90	91.2	-113.0	-21.8	-23.4	-45.2
1887-91	94.7	-115.9	-21.2	-25.1	-46.3
1888-92	99.8	-119.0	-19.2	-27.4	-46.6
1889-93	105.2	-121.5	-16.3	-29.0	-45.3
1890-94	109.6	-120.9	-11.3	-31.0	-42.3
1891-95	113.5	-119.5	-6.0	-32.0	-38.0
1892-96	118.2	-118.5	-0.3	-32.7	-33.0
1893-97	125.2	-118.7	6.5	-33.2	-26.7
1894-98	133.9	-123.7	10.2	-33.9	-23.7
1895-99	145.9	-135.6	10.3	-33.0	-22.7

Source. Penelope Hartland, "Canadian Balance," p. 726, Table 3.
Note: Minus signs indicate debit items. Export and import figures
are based on f.o.b. valuations and include gold.

about $200 million, four-fifths of which represented
British holdings of Canadian provincial and railroad
bonds. The components were as follows:

British holdings of provincial bonds	$70 million
British holdings of railroad securities	90
Other British investments	25
United States direct investments	15
Total	$200 million

Between 1867 and the end of the century, this total grew more than five-fold. The largest absolute increase was in British holdings of publicly issued Canadian securities (again, mostly government and railroad bonds), but the growth in United States direct investment was also marked. Hartland gives the following direct estimate of the net increase in Canadian indebtedness from 1868 to the end of 1899:

Public security sales	$789 million
United States direct investment and private security sales	191
British direct investment and private security sales	90
Investment by all other countries	35
Total	$1,105 million

These figures are net of retirements and redemptions; the total foreign investment in Canada at the turn of the century was, therefore, a little over $1.3 billion.

In the years from Confederation to the end of the century, therefore, Canada absorbed more than one billion dollars of foreign capital. Despite the fact that this period saw the construction of the Canadian Pacific Railway and the opening-up (though not the large-scale settlement) of the Canadian west, it is generally considered a phase of slow growth, if not of stagnation, in Canadian economic history. Certainly it was a period of generally falling prices and some commercial distress. Aggregate statistics, however, show a not unsatisfactory rate of growth for these years: Gross national product at constant prices grew at an average rate of about 3 per cent per year between 1870 and 1890.[9] It would not be far from the truth to describe it as a period of frustration and disappointment, when growth rates were less than had been hoped for and expected.

TABLE 3

United States Foreign Investments, 1897

Area	Direct (US$ millions)	Per cent	Direct and portfolio (US$ millions)	Per cent
Europe	131.0	20.6	151.0	22.0
Canada and Newfoundland	159.7	25.3	189.7	27.8
Cuba and other West Indies	49.0	7.7	49.0	7.2
Mexico	200.2	31.5	200.2	29.2
Central America	21.2	3.3	21.2	3.1
South America	37.9	6.0	37.9	5.5
Africa	1.0	0.2	1.0	0.1
Asia	23.0	3.6	23.0	3.4
Oceania	1.5	0.2	1.5	0.2
International, including banking	10.0	1.6	10.0	1.5
Totals	634.5	100.0	684.5	100.0

Source. Cleona Lewis, *International Investments*, p. 606, Tables II and III.

Note: Percentages have been rounded to the nearest tenth of a point.

To finance railroad construction, both in the 1850's and later, Canada relied heavily on the sale of bonds (governmental and corporate, the latter usually with a government guarantee) to investors in other countries. Most of this portfolio investment came from Great Britain. Some Canadian bonds appear to have been sold in the United States also, but most United States investment in

Canada was, from the beginning, direct investment, for example, the purchase of land, timber or mineral rights, and the establishment of branch plants and corporate subsidiaries. This type of investment increased from about $15 million in 1867 to around $160 million at the end of 1899. By the end of the nineteenth century, only Mexico, Canada's southern counterpart, had a larger share of the total. Cleona Lewis, estimating the size of United States investment in other countries as of the year 1897, presents the figures shown in Table 3.[10]

Classified by type of activity, United States direct investments in Canada were distributed as shown in Table 4.

TABLE 4

United States Direct Investments in Canada, 1897, by Type of Activity

Activity	Total direct investment (US$ millions)	Per cent
Selling organizations	10	6.25
Mining and smelting		
Precious metals and precious stones	30	18.8
Industrial minerals, excluding oil	25	15.7
Oil production and distribution	6	3.75
Agriculture	18	11.3
Manufacturing		
Pulp and paper	20	12.5
Other	35	21.9
Railroads	12.7	7.95
Public utilities	2	1.25
Miscellaneous	1	0.6
Totals	159.7	100.00

Source. Cleona Lewis, *International Investments*, pp. 578 ff.
Note: The "miscellaneous" figure represents an arbitrary allocation of certain totals not distributed by country, such as ocean shipping, freight handling, purchasing, and banking.

With the beginning of the twentieth century, we enter upon a period that has received the most thorough attention, largely as a result of the brilliant pioneering work of Professor Jacob Viner.[11] First, as to the aggregates: Table 5 gives, in summary form, estimates of Canada's balance of payments on current account from 1900 to 1913. The figures are essentially Viner's, but include certain corrections and recalculations by Hartland.[12]

TABLE 5

Canada: Summary Balance of Payments on Current Account, 1900–13
(millions of dollars)

Year	Commodity exports	Commodity imports	Balance on commodity account	Balance on other current items	Net balance on current account
1900	184.9	−189.3	−4.4	−31.4	−35.8
1901	205.2	−192.6	12.6	−31.8	−19.2
1902	215.9	−212.8	3.1	−29.5	−26.4
1903	226.8	−265.3	−38.5	−30.6	−69.2
1904	198.1	−256.8	−58.7	−31.4	−90.2
1905	229.1	−269.2	−40.1	−41.7	−81.8
1906	267.6	−329.6	−62.0	−47.5	−109.4
1907	271.3	−392.5	−121.2	−61.8	−183.0
1908	268.1	−312.6	−44.5	−78.1	−122.5
1909	288.7	−361.9	−73.2	−74.5	−147.7
1910	296.6	−450.4	−153.8	−80.6	−234.4
1911	301.6	−543.2	−241.6	−96.3	−337.9
1912	375.7	−651.2	−275.5	−143.2	−418.7
1913	471.4	−694.2	−222.8	−177.6	−400.4

Source. Penelope Hartland, "Canadian Balance," p. 749, Table A-2.
Note: Minus signs indicate debit items. Individual items do not always add to totals because of rounding.

For the period 1900 through 1913, the net inflow of capital into Canada, allowing for Canadian capital exports, may be estimated at $2,277 million. The corresponding gross figure is $2,414 million.[13] In these fourteen years, therefore, Canada absorbed more than twice as much foreign capital as in the entire period from Confederation through 1899. The geographical sources of the inflow are estimated by Viner as shown in Table 6.[14]

TABLE 6

Investments of Foreign Countries in Canada, 1900–13
(thousands of dollars)

Year	British	United States	Other countries	Total
1900	10,068	17,907	3,745	31,720
1901	15,085	18,339	3,745	37,169
1902	11,916	23,358	7,060	42,334
1903	28,833	22,093	3,745	54,671
1904	29,500	25,780	6,618	61,898
1905	76,398	32,408	3,745	112,551
1906	68,453	29,510	7,293	105,256
1907	65,251	25,992	3,845	95,088
1908	181,404	32,744	7,982	222,130
1909	212,725	36,153	4,522	253,400
1910	218,457	72,664	22,065	313,186
1911	244,427	76,143	27,840	348,410
1912	214,830	81,735	24,550	321,115
1913	375,771	134,968	35,960	546,699
Totals	1,753,118	629,794	162,715	2,545,627

Source. Jacob Viner, *Canada's Balance*, p. 139, Table XLIV.

Over the fourteen-year period, Great Britain provided about 69 per cent of the total inflow, and the United States almost 25 per cent. The British share of the total was greater toward the end of the period, rising from just under 41 per cent in the first five-year period to just over 71 per cent in the last. That of the United States declined from approximately 47 per cent to approximately 22 per cent in the same two periods.

Investments in Canada by Britain and by the United States differed not only in volume but also in form. Portfolio investment was once again characteristic of the in-

flow from Britain, and direct investment of the inflow
from the United States (Table 7).

TABLE 7

Foreign Investments in Canada, by Type, 1900–13
(thousands of dollars)

Type	Great Britain	United States	Other
Securities			
Public issues	1,433,884	134,213	} 62,715
Private sales	63,755	100,000	
Treasury bills	23,000	—	—
Miscellaneous			
Insurance companies	32,479	50,251	} 100,000
Other miscellaneous	200,000	345,330	
Totals	1,753,118	629,794	162,715

Source. Jacob Viner, *Canada's Balance*, p. 126, Table XXXVIII;
p. 134, Table XLI; p. 138, Table XLIII.

The category "other miscellaneous" in Table 7 refers to
direct investments in Canada: the purchase of Canadian
mining, agricultural, timber, and urban properties; the
investments of foreign shipping companies in Canadian
coastwise and internal shipping; the purchase or establishment of branch plants and subsidiaries; foreign funds
lent on mortgage in Canada; and foreign capital used in
financing Canadian import and export trade. There are
no comprehensive data for such investments beyond
certain estimates presented by F. W. Field, editor of
The Monetary Times, in 1911 and 1914, and these are
probably incomplete.[15] Nevertheless, the evidence indicates clearly the preponderance of direct investment in
the capital inflow from the United States, as contrasted
with security sales in the inflow from Great Britain. Direct
investments, by these estimates, accounted for almost
55 per cent of United States investment in Canada between 1900 and 1913, but only about 11 per cent of
British investment.

The total stock of foreign capital in Canada at the end of 1913, on the basis of Viner's estimates, was $3,745.6 million, or more than three times the 1900 total.[16] Of this, $2,793.1 million, or almost three-quarters, represented the accumulated value of British investment; the United States had accounted for $779.8 million, or a little over one-fifth. Canada by this time had been the recipient of 13.7 per cent of all the foreign investments of the United Kingdom, the United States had received 20 per cent of the outflow from the same source, and Latin America had received 20.1 per cent.[17] Clearly, in the years after 1900 Canada had found herself in the mainstream of the international flow of capital.

The inflow from the United States in this period grew faster than that from Britain, though it was much smaller in absolute size. By 1913, the value of United States in-

TABLE 8

United States Foreign Investments, 1914

Area	Direct (US$ millions)	Per cent	Direct and portfolio (US$ millions)	Per cent
Europe	573.3	21.7	691.8	19.7
Canada and Newfoundland	618.4	23.4	867.2	24.7
Cuba and other West Indies	281.3	10.6	336.3	9.6
Mexico	587.1	22.2	853.5	24.3
Central America	89.6	3.4	93.2	2.6
South America	323.1	12.3	365.7	10.4
Africa	13.0	0.5	13.2	0.35
Asia	119.5	4.5	245.9	7.0
Oceania	17.0	0.6	17.0	0.45
International, including banking	30.0	0.8	30.0	0.9
Totals	2,652.3	100.0	3,513.8	100.00

Source. Cleona Lewis, *International Investments*, p. 606, Tables II and III.

vestments in Canada was more than 4½ times what it had been in 1900, while the value of British investments had grown only 2½ times. Statistics of American foreign investments in this period show, indeed, that tendencies already evident in 1900 had become accentuated (Table 8). Canada by 1914 had received more United States investment than any other part of the world, though Mexico was not far behind.

TABLE 9

United States Direct Investments in Canada, 1914, by Type of Activity

Activity	Total direct investment (US$ millions)	Per cent
Selling organizations	27.0	4.4
Mining and smelting		
Precious metals and precious stones	56.5	9.1
Industrial minerals, excluding oil	102.5	16.5
Oil production and distribution	25.0	4.0
Agriculture	101.0	16.3
Manufacturing		
Pulp and paper	74.0	12.0
Other	147.0	23.8
Railroads	68.9	11.2
Public utilities	8.0	1.3
Miscellaneous	8.5	1.4
Totals	618.4	100.0

Source. Cleona Lewis, *International Investments*, pp. 578 *ff.*
Note: The figure for agriculture includes speculative land holdings, and timber lands not held by pulp and paper companies.

Of the total United States direct investment in Canada and Newfoundland of US$618.4 million, more than a quarter had been invested in the production of industrial minerals (excluding oil) and pulp and paper; slightly less than a quarter had gone into the development of manufacturing other than pulp and paper. The breakdown by sectors is shown in Table 9.

The gap between Viner's estimates for the period 1900–13 and the start of the official Dominion Bureau of Statistics series in 1926 has been bridged by Professor Frank A. Knox. The intervention of the first World War adds to this period special difficulties of estimation, and it would be unwise to place much confidence in the estimates for any single year. Nevertheless, the trends stand out with some clarity, and in particular the reversal after 1914 of the inflow of capital that had sustained the Canadian economy in its prewar boom. Once again, we may begin with a summary view of the Canadian balance of payments in this period. Table 10 presents Professor Knox's estimates.

An indirect estimate of Canada's net capital imports

TABLE 10

Canada: Summary Balance of Payments on Current Account, 1914–25
(millions of dollars)

Year	Com-modity exports	Com-modity imports	Balance on commodity account	Balance on other current items[a]	Net balance on current account
1914	369.1	−470.8	−101.7	−186.5	−288.2
1915	613.9	−447.2	166.7	−224.0	−57.3
1916	1,072.4	−762.4	310.0	−287.1	22.9
1917	1,555.2	−996.5	558.7	−382.7	176.0
1918	1,209.4	−922.4	287.0	−368.8	−81.8
1919	1,261.7	−951.4	310.3	−260.0	50.3
1920	1,267.1	−1,428.7	−161.6	−161.8	−323.4
1921	800.4	−827.8	−27.4	−129.8	−157.2
1922	884.1	−744.6	139.5	−186.9	−47.4
1923	1,003.9	−885.1	118.8	−68.7	50.1
1924	1,032.6	−789.9	242.7	−105.2	137.5
1925	1,241.1	−872.4	368.7	−95.5	273.2

Source. Frank A. Knox, *Dominion Monetary Policy* (Ottawa, 1939), p. 89.

[a] Includes gold trade balance.

Note: Minus signs indicate debit items.

over this twelve-year period, based on the balance of
payments on current account, would amount to only
$245.3 million, capital imports of $955.3 million in six
years being offset by capital exports of $710.0 million in
the other six. The contrast with the more than $2 billion
of net capital imports in the preceding fourteen years is,
of course, striking, and it indicates a very marked change
in Canada's status as an international borrower. Direct
estimates of Canada's borrowings in this period, however,
do not entirely confirm this impression; they show a
substantially greater net inflow of capital than the balance
of payments on current account would indicate. Knox's
direct estimates of the net movement of capital are as
shown in Table 11.

TABLE 11

Net Foreign Investment in Canada, 1914–25
(millions of dollars)

Year	Net new security issues or retirements (−)	Net sales of outstanding securities	Net change in external assets of Canadian banks	Other capital movements (including direct investment)	Net movement of capital
1914	298.1	−3.0	21.2	25.5	341.8
1915	179.0	−5.0	−113.4	60.8	121.4
1916	254.2	−8.0	−129.4	−44.4	72.4
1917	126.9	−10.0	10.8	−100.7	27.0
1918	−12.8	−10.0	−28.5	−113.0	−164.3
1919	25.1	−40.0	−21.7	5.3	−31.3
1920	153.7	−55.0	42.4	44.5	185.6
1921	123.6	−40.0	144.4	54.0	282.0
1922	210.3	−20.0	27.0	46.8	264.1
1923	109.6	−40.0	−12.7	72.8	129.7
1924	143.0	−50.0	−15.7	20.3	97.6
1925	13.0	−80.0	−92.8	16.5	−143.3

Source. Frank A. Knox, *Monetary Policy*, pp. 92–93. *Cf.* Penelope
Hartland, "Canadian Balance," p. 752, Table A-4.
Note: Minus signs indicate a net outflow.

The figures given in Table 11 indicate a net inflow of capital over the period amounting to no less than $1,182.7 million, which is uncomfortably greater than the total indicated by the current account. Nothing that has been suggested so far seems to explain the paradox in a completely satisfactory manner. Hartland suggests that Knox's estimates of the net purchases of outstanding securities by Canadians may be too low by 100 per cent or more, arguing that "Canadians were making unprecedently large purchases of foreign securities in these years [the 1920's], especially in New York." [18] No supporting evidence is provided, however. There is also the possibility of error in the current account items. John Stovel, for example, suggests that the estimated net credit to Canada for tourist expenditures may be too large by 50 per cent, and furthermore that the estimated debit on account of immigrants' remittances may be too small.[19] If correct, these modifications would reduce the discrepancy, but they would not eliminate it completely.

The source of the discrepancy may well lie in the estimates of the outflow of capital from Canada. If so, greater confidence can be placed in Knox's estimate of the increase in Canada's gross foreign indebtedness than in his estimate of the net inflow. The total stock of foreign (including British) capital invested in Canada grew, according to Knox's calculations, from $3,836.9 million at the end of 1914 to $5,714.1 million at the end of 1925, an increase of almost 50 per cent.[20] Of the total at the end of the period, 25 per cent was invested in government securities; 36.5 per cent in public utilities (including railroads); 28.4 per cent in industry; and the remainder in merchandising, insurance, finance, agriculture, and miscellaneous services.[21]

The increase in the total stock of foreign capital over

the period was due entirely to the growth of United States investments; the value of British investments fell during these years, as a result of repatriation and liquidation of debt, from $2,778.5 million to $2,345.7 million and that of all other countries from $177.7 million to $149.2 million. United States investment, on the other hand, grew from $880.7 million at the end of 1914 to $3,219.2 million at the end of 1925, an increase of 265½ per cent which for the first time made the United States rather than Britain Canada's principal foreign creditor. This remarkable growth in the value of United States investment in Canada reflected partly the diversion of Canadian governmental and corporate borrowing from London to New York after the outbreak of World War I and the liquidation of British dollar investments for the purchase of war material; but the change in the relative importance of British and United States investment in Canada was no short-term phenomenon. British investments in Canada never regained their relative position; in dollar value, it was not until 1957 that they exceeded the level reached in 1916, the previous peak year.[22]

Lewis' independent calculation of the size of the United States investment in Canada in 1924 gives a total smaller than that suggested by Knox for the same year, probably because of a conservative estimate of direct investments (Table 12). The comparison with other countries and the breakdown by sector is, however, informative. Total United States investment in Europe was by this date slightly larger than the corresponding figure for Canada, chiefly because of the flood of dollar loans floated in New York in the war and postwar years. Direct United States investment in Canada, however, was still greater than that in any other category, though smaller than direct investment in Latin America as a whole.

TABLE 12

United States Foreign Investments, 1924

Area	Direct (US$ millions)	Per cent	Direct and portfolio (US$ millions)	Per cent
Europe	921.3	17.1	2,652.8	26.8
Canada and Newfoundland	1,080.5	20.0	2,631.7	26.4
Cuba and other West Indies	993.2	18.4	1,101.3	11.1
Mexico	735.4	13.7	1,005.1	10.0
Central America	143.5	2.6	155.3	1.5
South America	947.1	17.6	1,411.2	14.2
Africa	58.5	1.1	58.7	0.6
Asia	267.2	5.0	671.8	6.7
Oceania	117.0	2.2	140.7	1.4
International, including banking	125.0	2.3	125.0	1.3
Totals[a]	5,388.7	100.0	9,953.6	100.0

Source. Cleona Lewis, *International Investments*, p. 606, Tables II and III.

[a] Excluding short-term credits.

Analysis of the sectoral distribution of United States direct investment in Canada reveals the now-familiar concentration on industrial raw materials and secondary manufacturing (Table 13). These two categories (including pulp and paper) accounted for more than 70 per cent of the total in 1924, as compared with slightly over 50 per cent in 1914.

For the years after 1926, there are available official Dominion Bureau of Statistics estimates of Canada's balance of payments on current and capital account. Statistics for the period from 1926 to the outbreak of the second World War in 1939, as might be expected,

TABLE 13

United States Direct Investments in Canada, 1924, by Type of Activity

Activity	Total direct investment (US$ millions)	Per cent
Selling organizations	35.0	3.2
Mining and smelting		
Precious metals and precious stones	66.5	6.1
Industrial minerals, excluding oil	158.0	14.6
Oil production and distribution	40.0	3.7
Agriculture	30.0	2.8
Manufacturing		
Pulp and paper	180.0	16.8
Other	420.0	38.8
Railroads	79.0	7.3
Public utilities	30.0	2.8
Miscellaneous	42.0	3.9
Totals	1,080.5	100.0

Source. Cleona Lewis, *International Investments*, pp. 578 *ff*.
Note: Agriculture includes farms and timber not held by pulp and paper companies.

reflect very strongly the impact of the depression. Canada's balance of payments on current account, already unfavorable in 1927, became even more so in 1929 and 1930, exports falling initially more quickly than imports; by 1934, however, the current balance had turned favorable — a characteristic feature of the Canadian economy in depression.[23] Imports of capital, which had been large in 1929 and 1930, later tapered off sharply, and for the last seven years of our period (1933 onward) Canada was on balance exporting capital. The balance of payments on current account for this period is summarized in Table 14.

TABLE 14

Canada: Summary Balance of Payments on Current Account, 1926–39
(millions of dollars)

Year	Commodity exports	Commodity imports	Balance on commodity account	Balance on other current items[a]	Net balance on current account
1926	1,272	−973	299	−172	127
1927	1,215	−1,057	158	−168	−10
1928	1,341	−1,209	132	−164	−32
1929	1,178	−1,272	−94	−217	−311
1930	880	−973	−93	−244	−337
1931	601	−580	21	−195	−174
1932	495	−398	97	−193	−96
1933	532	−368	164	−166	−2
1934	648	−484	164	−96	68
1935	732	−526	206	−81	125
1936	954	−612	342	−98	244
1937	1,041	−776	265	−85	180
1938	844	−649	195	−95	100
1939	906	−713	193	−67	126

Source. Dominion Bureau of Statistics, *Canadian Balance, 1926 to 1948*, p. 154, Table III, and p. 158, Table VII.

[a] Includes net exports of nonmonetary gold.

Note: Minus signs indicate debit items.

The cumulative annual balances on current account indicate that over the period as a whole there was a net export of capital of $8.0 million, the large positive balances in the last six years more than offsetting the negative balances of the earlier ones.[24] Direct estimates of the net capital flow confirm the fact of an export of capital on balance but yield a somewhat larger total: $30.8 million. Discrepancies between the two estimates, however, are not as serious as for the 1914–25 period. The direct estimates are given in Table 15.

TABLE 15

Net Foreign Investment in Canada, 1926–39
(millions of dollars)

Year	Net new security issues or retirements (−)	Net sales of outstanding securities	Net change in external assets of Canadian banks	Other capital movements (including direct investment)	Net movement of capital
1926	161.0	−135.0	−51.8	28.6	2.8
1927	141.0	−171.0	16.0	24.0	10.0
1928	7.0	−126.0	87.0	64.0	32.0
1929	147.0	−2.0	88.0	78.0	311.0
1930	290.0	56.0	—	−9.0	337.0
1931	−2.0	45.0	28.0	103.0	174.0
1932	−1.0	85.0	38.0	−26.0	96.0
1933	−32.0	51.0	24.0	−54.0	−11.0
1934	−58.0	9.0	−19.0	−46.0	−114.0
1935	−139.0	51.0	—	−64.0	−152.0
1936	−164.0	8.0	3.0	−88.0	−241.0
1937	−80.0	−5.0	−13.0	−74.0	−172.0
1938	−62.0	29.0	−7.0	−66.0	−106.0
1939	−96.0	82.0	—	−122.0	−136.0

Source. Dominion Bureau of Statistics, *Canadian Balance, 1926 to 1948*, p. 163, Table XII, and p. 168, Table XVII. Estimates for 1926 are from Frank A. Knox, *Monetary Policy*, pp. 92–93; the estimate of net change in external bank assets for the year 1938 is from J. A. Stovel, *Canada*, p. 343, Table 27.

Note: Minus signs indicate a net outflow. Statistics of net sales of outstanding securities are estimated for 1927–32 and recorded thereafter.

The total stock of foreign capital invested in Canada increased, according to the official estimates, from $6,002.6 million in 1926 to $7,613.8 million in 1930 and then declined to $7,364.5 million in 1933 and to $6,913.3 million in 1939.[25] British investment fell over the period by some $160 million, or from 44 per cent of the total to 36 per cent, while United States investment increased by approximately $955 million, or from 53.2 per cent of the aggregate to 60 per cent. The sectoral distribution of the investments of Great Britain and the United States at the beginning and end of the period is shown in Table 16.

TABLE 16

British and United States Investments in Canada, 1926 and 1939,
by Type of Investment
(percentages)

Type	British		United States	
	1926	1939	1926	1939
Government securities	19.3	18.4	28.5	29.5
Public utilities				
Railroads	52.0	49.2	16.0	14.2
Other	3.7	3.6	9.0	10.4
Manufacturing	8.9	10.3	29.8	28.0
Mining and smelting	1.9	2.5	5.2	6.0
Merchandising	1.9	2.2	3.1	3.1
Financial institutions	6.6	8.9	3.9	4.8
Other enterprises	0.2	0.1	1.9	1.5
Miscellaneous assets	5.5	4.8	2.6	2.5
Totals	100.0	100.0	100.0	100.0

Source. Dominion Bureau of Statistics, *Canadian Balance, 1926 to 1948*, pp. 181–182, Tables XXXIII, XXXIV, and XXXV.

The reduction in British investment took place principally through the sale and redemption of government and railroad securities, both of which were smaller absolutely and as a proportion of the total in 1939 than in 1926. British investment in Canadian manufacturing, mining and smelting, and financial institutions, in contrast, increased both absolutely and relatively, although it should be noted that in each of these classes the dollar value of the investment declined in the shorter period 1930–39. United States investment in Canadian manufacturing, on the other hand, accounted for a smaller share of the total in 1939 than in 1926, although in dollar value it was somewhat higher. The most significant absolute and relative increase was in United States investment in Canadian government bonds, which grew throughout the whole period.

No analysis is available of the geographical distribution of United States foreign investments in the immediate prewar years. There is, however, Lewis' survey for 1935 and a United States Department of Commerce survey of direct investments for 1936. To facilitate comparisons with earlier periods, Lewis' estimates are presented in Table 17.

TABLE 17

United States Foreign Investments, 1935

Area	Direct (US$ millions)	Per cent	Direct and portfolio (US$ millions)	Per cent
Europe	1,369.6	19.0	3,026.0	23.5
Canada and Newfoundland	1,692.4	23.5	3,657.6	28.6
Cuba and other West Indies	731.3	10.1	871.7	6.8
Mexico	651.7	9.0	912.9	7.1
Central America	160.0	2.2	192.0	1.5
South America	1,718.2	23.8	2,574.4	20.0
Africa	123.6	1.7	125.8	1.0
Asia	487.6	6.8	915.3	7.1
Oceania	159.8	2.2	413.1	3.2
International, including banking	125.0	1.7	151.9	1.2
Totals[a]	7,219.2	100.0	12,840.7	100.0

Source. Cleona Lewis, *International Investments*, p. 606, Tables II and III.

[a] Excluding short-term credits.

The Department of Commerce estimate for 1936, which
sets total United States direct investment abroad at
US$6,690.5 million, allocates 29.2 per cent of the total to
Canada, as compared with Lewis' 23.5 per cent for Canada
and Newfoundland combined, and 42.6 per cent to Latin
America, as compared with a total of 35 per cent for the
three corresponding areas in Lewis' table. Whichever set
of figures is regarded as the more reliable, the concentration of United States direct investment in Canada and
Latin America is clear. The sectoral distribution of this
investment shows an emphasis on transportation and on
mining and smelting in both areas. Direct investment in
manufacturing was, however, much more important in
the case of Canada, and investment in agriculture (principally tropical fruits, sugar, and coffee) more important in
Latin America (Table 18).

TABLE 18

*United States Direct Investments in Canada and Latin America, 1936,
by Industry*

Industry	Canada Total (US$ millions)	Per cent	Latin America Total (US$ millions)	Per cent
Agriculture	10.4	0.5	400.4	14.1
Mining and smelting	238.8	12.3	708.2	24.8
Petroleum	108.1	5.5	452.6	15.9
Manufacturing	799.0	41.0	191.8	6.8
Transportation, communica- tion, and public utilities	519.9	26.7	937.1	32.9
Trade	78.5	4.0	100.0	3.5
Miscellaneous (including finance and insurance)	196.8	10.0	56.9	2.0
All industries	1,951.6	100.0	2,847.0	100.0

Source. U.S. Dept. of Commerce, *Foreign Investments of the United
States* (Washington, D.C., 1953), p. 49, Appendix Table 13.
Note: Details may not add to totals because of rounding to nearest
tenth of a million.

A survey made by the Dominion Bureau of Statistics and used by Herbert Marshall and his associates for their investigation of Canadian-American industry provides additional information on the industrial distribution of United States direct investment in Canada, on its relative importance in different sectors, and on the minority non-American (chiefly Canadian) interest in United States firms then operating in Canada. The figures (Table 19) refer to the year 1932; "capital employed" excludes depreciation reserves, marketable securities, advances to affiliates, and so on, and would therefore normally be

TABLE 19

United States-Controlled and United States-Affiliated Companies Operating in Canada, 1932

Industry	Number of firms	Capital employed		Gross value of products[a]	
		Total (thousands)	Per cent non-U.S. minority interest	Total, these firms (thousands)	Per cent of Canadian total
Manufacturing	805	$833,293	14.16	$455,900	23.73
Mining	49	236,599	30.00	67,150	38.71
Utilities	81	707,751	33.02	94,405	17.90
Merchandising (1930)	203	291,725	15.90	636,307	—
Miscellaneous	39	37,882	37.20	23,667	—
Estimated direct investments in agricultural and timber lands, summer homes, insurance buildings, etc.	—	60,000	—	—	—
Totals	1,177	$2,167,250	22.29	—	—

Source. Herbert Marshall *et al.*, *Canadian-American Industry*, p. 25, Table V.

[a] Gross incomes for public utilities, merchandising, and miscellaneous companies.

smaller than the book value of assets, the concept more frequently used.

These figures indicate both the wide spread of United States direct investment in Canada in this period and the substantial fractions of Canadian output for which United States-controlled and -affiliated firms were already responsible. Almost one-quarter of Canadian manufacturing output (by gross value of product) and more than two-fifths of Canadian mining output originated in United States-controlled firms at this date. Clearly, United States capital had already established itself firmly in the manufacturing sector of the Canadian economy.

The stock of United States capital invested in Canada at the end of 1939 was $4,151 million, or 60 per cent of all nonresident investment in Canada at that time. By the end of 1958, it had risen to $14,600 million, or 77 per cent of the total, having risen in each of the intervening years.[26] In 1939, United States interests controlled 32 per cent of Canadian manufacturing and 38 per cent of Canadian mining and smelting; by 1957, the corresponding ratios had risen to 43 per cent and 52 per cent.[27] The trends already discussed, in short, have continued unabated in the years from 1939 to the present, and this despite the fact that during this period Canada has been, in some years, a net exporter of capital on a very large scale.

The Canadian balance of payments on current account for these years is summarized in Table 20. Two characteristics stand out clearly: Canada's large favorable balance during the war and immediate postwar years, and the large unfavorable balance in most of the years since then. The explanation for the favorable balance is to be found in Canada's official contributions to war finance and to postwar reconstruction and defense. The unfavorable balance since 1950 reflects the very large inward move-

TABLE 20

Canada: Summary Balance of Payments on Current Account, 1940–58

Year	Com- modity exports	Com- modity imports	Balance on commodity account	Balance on other current items[a]	Net balance on current account
1940	1,202	−1,006	196	−47	149
1941	1,732	−1,264	468	23	491
1942	2,515	−1,406	1,109	−8	1,101
1943	3,050	−1,579	1,471	−265	1,206
1944	3,590	−1,398	2,192	−1,174	1,018
1945	3,474	−1,442	2,032	−486	1,546
1946	2,393	−1,822	571	−208	363
1947	2,723	−2,535	188	−139	49
1948	3,030	−2,598	432	19	451
1949	2,989	−2,696	293	−116	177
1950	3,139	−3,129	10	−344	−334
1951	3,950	−4,097	−147	−370	−517
1952	4,339	−3,850	489	−339	150
1953	4,152	−4,210	−58	−385	−443
1954	3,929	−3,916	13	−445	−432
1955	4,332	−4,543	−211	−487	−698
1956	4,837	−5,565	−728	−638	−1,366
1957	4,909	−5,488	−579	−845	−1,424
1958	4,890	−5,060	−170	−915	−1,085

Source. Dominion Bureau of Statistics, *Canadian Balance, 1926 to 1948*, p. 158, Table VII; and D.B.S., *Canadian Balance, 1958*, p. 46, Table II.

[a] Includes gold production available for export and official contributions.

Note: Minus signs indicate debit items.

ment of United States capital — and to some extent other foreign capital — during a period of rapid growth.

Statistics of the net movement of capital confirm the evidence for heavy external borrowings in the period 1950–58 as contrasted with large outflows of capital in the earlier years.[28] Primarily responsible for the massive exports of capital during the war years were Canadian contributions to mutual aid to the allied powers and a special contribution of $1,000 million made to the United Kingdom for the purchase of war supplies in Canada in 1942. Extensive repatriations of Canadian securities owned in the United Kingdom also reflected the pressures of war finance and added to the capital outflow. Capital imports during the period 1950–58 were obtained from two major sources: the issue of new Canadian securities in the United States and direct investments, also largely from the United States. Table 21 gives a summary of capital flows from 1940 to the end of 1958.

Over the whole nineteen-year period, Canada was on balance a capital exporter, accumulating claims against other countries to the extent of $452 million. The total, however, obscures two quite different phases. During the first decade of the period, there was a net outward movement of capital of $6,587 million; during the last nine years, there was a net inward movement of $6,135 million. The war and immediate postwar years, in fact, constituted a distinctive phase in Canada's balance-of-payments experience. That such large capital exports could be generated when called for reflected the strength of the Canadian economy and the maturity of its fiscal and monetary institutions. But the change to the status of large-scale international lender in this period did not mean that Canada was now generating more savings than could profitably be employed in the domestic economy or that investment opportunities in a commercial sense were more attractive abroad. It meant simply that Canada had undertaken to supply a major share of the resources necessary for the conflict in which she was engaged and for the reconstruction that followed. The resumption of heavy capital imports in the early 1950's reflected a return to the historic pattern of Canadian development: growth achieved by the application of sophisticated technology to

TABLE 21

Net Foreign Investment in Canada, 1940-58
(millions of dollars)

Year	Net new Canadian security issues or retirements (−)	Net sales of outstanding Canadian securities	Direct investment in Canada[a]	Other capital movements	Net movement of capital[b]
1940	−191	5	—	−2	−188
1941	−229	38	—	−306	−497
1942	−351	148	—	−905	−1,108
1943	−176	272	—	−1,291	−1,195
1944	−108	198	—	−1,098	−1,008
1945	−120	351	—	−1,782	−1,551
1946	−321	194	40	−276	−363
1947	−269	−13	61	172	−49
1948	36	3	71	−561	−451
1949	−42	8	94	−237	−177
1950	−74	329	222	−143	334
1951	227	38	309	−57	517
1952	227	−94	346	−643	−164
1953	189	−31	426	−141	443
1954	128	63	392	−151	432
1955	−18	−27	417	326	698
1956	526	199	583	58	1,366
1957	665	92	514	153	1,424
1958	519	91	420	55	1,085

Source. Dominion Bureau of Statistics, *Canadian Balance, 1926 to 1948*, p. 168, Table XVII; D.B.S., *Canadian Balance, 1958*, p. 46, Table II. Figures for 1958 from Bank of Canada, *Annual Report of the Governor to the Minister of Finance, 1959*, p. 25.

[a] Included in Other Capital Movements, 1940–45.

[b] Including change in official holdings of gold, sterling, and U.S. dollars.

Note: Minus signs denote an outflow.

virgin resources, with the aid of capital borrowed from more advanced areas.

The total stock of foreign capital invested in Canada grew between 1939 and the end of 1958 from $6.9 billion to $19.1 billion, an increase of more than 170 per cent.[29] Of this increase, the United States contributed $10.4 billion, the United Kingdom $0.6 billion, and all other countries a little over $1.1 billion. Of the total United States investment in Canada in 1958, 63 per cent was direct investment, the remainder being portfolio and such miscellaneous investments as real estate and mortgages. The distribution by sectors at the end of 1957 is shown in Table 22, with the corresponding figures for 1939.

TABLE 22

United States Investments in Canada, 1939 and 1957, by Sectors

Sector	1939		1957	
	Amount ($ millions)	Per cent	Amount ($ millions)	Per cent
Government securities	1,221	29.4	2,059	15.4
Public utilities				
Railroads	588	14.1	489	3.6
Other (excluding pipelines)	432	10.7	471	3.5
Manufacturing	1,160	27.9	4,006	30.2
Mining and smelting (including petroleum and natural gas)	251	6.0	3,873	29.3
Merchandising	129	3.1	507	3.8
Financial institutions	201	4.8	1,200	9.1
Other enterprises	64	1.5	185	1.4
Miscellaneous assets	105	2.5	489	3.7
Totals	4,151	100.0	13,279	100.0

Source. Dominion Bureau of Statistics, *Canadian Balance, 1958*, p. 58, Table IX; and D.B.S., *Canada's International Investment Position, 1926–1954*, p. 78, Table VB.

Dominating the comparison between the two years is the remarkable increase in United States investment in the Canadian mineral industry. While investment in Canadian manufacturing rose by 250 per cent over the period and remained the largest single category in 1957, investment in Canadian minerals increased by no less than 1,543 per cent. Most of this increase reflected United States participation in Canadian petroleum and natural gas development after the important Leduc discovery in Alberta, but investment in other minerals was also significant, rising from $251 million in 1939 to $1,312 million at the end of 1957.

The United States was, at the end of 1958, by far the largest of Canada's foreign creditors. At the same time, more United States private capital had been invested in Canada by this date than in any other country. Preliminary estimates of the geographical distribution of United States private long-term foreign investments, as calculated by the U.S. Department of Commerce, are given in Table 23. Thirty-seven per cent of the total was invested in Canada, as compared with 26 per cent in Latin America, the next most important area of investment.

TABLE 23

United States Private Long-Term Foreign Investments, 1958, by Area
(US$ millions)

Type	All areas	West-ern Eu-rope	West-ern Euro-pean depend-encies	Other Eu-rope	Can-ada	Latin Ameri-can repub-lics	Other
Direct	27,075	4,382	1,038	—	8,929	8,730	3,996
Foreign dollar bonds	3,931	244	—	3	2,094	139	1,451
Other foreign securities	3,690	974	—	—	2,474	40	202
Other	2,640	1,114	25	19	345	860	277
Totals	37,336	6,714	1,063	22	13,842	9,769	5,926

Source. U.S. Dept. of Commerce, *Survey of Current Business*, August 1959, p. 29, Table 1.

We have surveyed the available estimates of Canada's capital imports and of the growth of the stock of foreign capital invested in Canada from the early nineteenth century to the present day. Questions can reasonably be raised about the homogeneity of the estimates in a statistical sense — whether they all measure the same thing — and about their reliability in view of the obvious uncertainties and ambiguities that characterize the earlier years. For our present purpose, however, which is to analyze long-run trends rather than year-to-year changes, these difficulties are not so serious as to make the endeavor pointless. Let us therefore put our various estimates together and see whether any reasonable impression emerges from them.

As regards the balance of payments on current account, from which we derive indirect estimates of the net inflow or outflow of capital, we have estimates in the form of five-year moving averages going back as far as 1868. If these are spliced to Viner's annual estimates for the period 1900–13, these to Knox's for the period 1914–26, and these to the D.B.S. figures from 1926 to the present day, we have a continuous series which, though it can hardly be called homogeneous in a statistical sense, at least illustrates the ebbs and flows of international capital out of and into Canada. This series is plotted in Chart I.[30] Excluding the two world wars when, as we have already seen, special factors impinged on the balance of payments, four subperiods seem to be evident: first, the long period of preparatory build-up from 1868 to the turn of the century, characterized by a relatively small but steady inflow of capital; second, the boom of 1900–13 with its large capital imports; third, the disturbed interwar period, marked by alternations of capital imports and exports, the flow being into Canada during periods of rising economic activity (1919–22 and 1927–30) and out of Canada

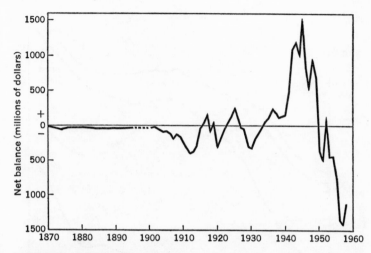

Chart I. Canada: Net Balance on Current Account, 1870–1958. Five-year Moving Averages: 1868–72 to 1895–99. Annual Totals: 1900–58.

in periods of recession; and fourth, the period from 1950 to the present, during which capital imports have been greater in dollar value than in any preceding period.

Turning now to the growth of the stock of foreign capital invested in Canada, we can, from the estimates already given and D.B.S. figures for more recent years, construct a series running with certain interruptions from 1900 to the present day. Estimates for periods earlier than 1900 are too incomplete for inclusion. Once again questions can be raised about the homogeneity of the series, and it must be admitted that, in years when different sets of estimates overlap, discrepancies do exist. The long-run trends, however, stand out with reasonable clarity. Chart II presents the totals from 1900 to 1958, and also the component series for the United States, Great Britain, and all other countries. Viner's estimates for the period

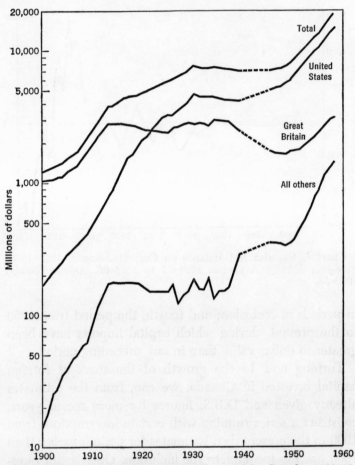

Chart II. Foreign Long-Term Capital Invested in Canada, 1900–58.

Source. Frank A. Knox, "Excursus," p. 299, Table A; Dominion Bureau of Statistics, *Canadian Balance: Methods and Results*, pp. 174–177, Table I; D.B.S., *Canadian Balance, 1958*, p. 61, Table XIII.

Note: Investments are valued at book value. Bonds and debentures are valued at par. Liabilities in foreign currencies are converted to Canadian dollars at the original par of exchange. For a number of years, between 1926 and 1937, the only available published figures are for capital employed. These have been adjusted to a book value basis by using book value estimates for 1926, 1930, and 1933, published by D.B.S., as bench-marks. No estimates are available for the years 1940 through 1944.

1900–13 are followed by Knox's for 1914–26, and these by D.B.S. estimates for 1927–39 and 1945 to 1958.

The total stock of foreign capital invested in Canada has, over the period covered, increased at an average rate of between 4½ and 5 per cent per year compounded. There have been two periods of rapid growth in the total stock (1900–13 and 1947 to the present), separated by one period of more moderate growth (1913–30) and one during which, as far as we can tell, the total stock was approximately constant (1930–47). From 1900 to 1913, the growth in the total reflected primarily growth in the stock of British capital, although American investment was also increasing rapidly. From 1913 on, the dominant influence is clearly United States investment. The value of British investments in Canada declined irregularly over the whole period from 1913 to 1948, a brief period of hesitant growth in the late 1920's having been more than offset by liquidations during two world wars. The contrast between the preponderance of British capital in the early years of the century and of United States capital since the 1920's stands out clearly.

It is tempting, on the basis of these statistics, to conclude that imports of foreign capital have been one of the major dynamic factors in Canadian economic development, and that the role of such capital imports in the Canadian economy is greater now than it has ever been in the past. Neither of these generalizations — whether true or false — can be proved or disproved solely on the basis of this kind of statistical evidence. The historical record reveals only a process of interaction between opportunities and resources, and a different kind of analysis is necessary before generalizations can be made with any confidence about the direction of causation. Similarly, it is true that the volume of imported capital has been much greater in recent years than in any previous periods. But Canada has in the meantime grown in size and complexity, and domestic supplies of capital have increased at least as much as external borrowings. One million dollars of imported capital does not exert the same leverage on the Canadian economy today as it did fifty years ago.

To appraise the relative importance of capital imports in the Canadian economy today with its importance in earlier periods the absolute figures must be converted into ratios. The simplest way to do this is to express the figures on a per capita basis, using population as a rough index of growth in the domestic economy. Hartland, for example, gives estimates for different periods, as shown in Table 24.

TABLE 24

Canada: Capital Imports Per Capita, Selected Periods

Year	Annual average
1869–73	$ 6.05
1895–99	4.41
1909–13	42.17
1946–50	−8.15
1951–55	12.97

Source. Penelope Hartland, "Canadian Balance," p. 720, Table 2.
Note: Minus sign denotes capital exports.

This at least serves as a useful corrective, suggesting that, large though the dollar volume of capital imports in recent years may appear, it is still considerably smaller than in previous periods of rapid development when population growth is taken into account. But we need to know more than this. If our interest is in the contribution of external capital to economic development, we should ideally be able to say what proportion of total investment expenditures foreign capital has been responsible for, and

this is far from easy. There is no simple way in which
financial transactions such as international transfers of
funds can be identified with investment in physical
assets.[31] Nevertheless, a variety of useful estimates have
been made.

The Dominion Bureau of Statistics now computes four
separate measures, each of which is designed to show in
a particular way the extent to which foreigners have
financed domestic investment in Canada.[32] Two of these
measure the extent to which Canada has on balance drawn
on or added to the resources of other countries, first in
terms of gross and secondly in terms of net investment.
The other two measures disregard outflows of capital
from Canada and concentrate on the question: To what
extent has foreign capital directly financed Canadian
investment?

We have, therefore, four estimates of the relative importance of foreign financing in Canadian capital formation. We may speak in terms of gross investment or net;
we may take outflows of capital into account or we may
ignore them. The resulting ratios are given in Table 25

TABLE 25

Foreign Financing of Canadian Investment, 1946–58
(percentages)

Measure	1946–49	1950–55	1956–58
Use of foreign resources as a percentage of:			
Gross capital formation	—	17	27
Net capital formation	−11	19	35
Direct foreign financing of:			
Gross capital formation	19	25	32
Net capital formation	24	33	44

Source. Dominion Bureau of Statistics, *Canadian Balance, 1958*,
p. 40, statement 20.
Note: Minus sign denotes net foreign investment by Canada.

for three postwar periods; Chart III presents the results graphically.

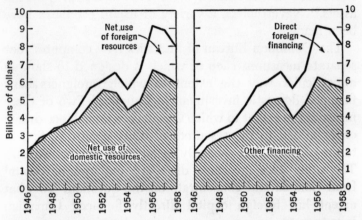

Chart III. Foreign Financing of Canadian Investment, 1946–58.

On the basis of these estimates, it is clear that the contribution of foreign capital to Canadian capital formation in recent years has been large, and that it has been growing larger. In the period 1950–55, foreign capital financed directly one-quarter of gross capital formation in Canada; in 1956–58 the percentage was almost one-third. In terms of net investment, the ratios are even higher. Comparisons with earlier periods in Canadian history are hazardous but essential for interpretation. In the period 1926–30, it has been estimated that the use of foreign resources as a percentage of net capital formation was about 25 per cent; direct foreign financing of net capital formation was about 50 per cent. In the period 1900–13, these ratios were probably even higher.[33] Canada's reliance on foreign capital in recent years has been great; but, to the best of our knowledge, it has not been greater than in previous periods of rapid growth.[34]

Furthermore, Canada's ability to carry her external debt has been growing. Net foreign indebtedness has increased steadily since 1949, reaching $13.0 billion at the end of 1958. The annual burden of servicing this debt, however, is considerably lighter than earlier in this century. This is shown in Table 26, in which Canada's

TABLE 26

Canada: Ratios of Interest and Dividend Payments to Nonresidents to Gross National Product and Receipts on Current Account, Selected Years, 1900–58

Period	Interest and dividend payments ($ millions)	Gross national product ($ millions)	Current receipts ($ millions)	Ratio 1 : 2 (per cent)	Ratio 1 : 3 (per cent)
	(1)	(2)	(3)		
1900	36	1,044	210	3.5	17.1
1910	92	2,186	388	4.2	23.7
1920	213	5,536	1,581	3.8	13.5
1926–29[a]	272	5,720	1,683	4.7	16.2
1930–38[a]	300	4,583	1,161	6.5	25.9
1939–45[a]	279	9,401	3,189	3.0	8.8
1946–50[a]	368	14,897	3,929	2.5	9.4
1951–55[a]	435	24,425	5,700	1.8	7.6
1956	523	30,098	6,621	1.7	7.9
1957	587	31,443	6,625	1.9	8.9
1958	586	32,630	6,565	1.8	8.8

Source. Gross National Product (GNP) estimates for 1900, 1910, and 1920 from O. J. Firestone, *Development*, p. 65, Table 9; other GNP figures from Dominion Bureau of Statistics, *National Accounts, Income and Expenditure, 1926–56*, pp. 32–33, Table 1, and subsequent publications; interest and dividend payments and current receipts from J. A. Stovel, *Canada*, pp. 338–345, Table 27, and D.B.S., *Canadian Balance, 1958*, p. 45, Table 1.

[a] Annual averages.

interest and dividend payments to nonresidents are compared first with the country's gross national product and then with her receipts on current account. Both ratios were relatively low at the end of 1958. By these tests, Canada's productivity and international earnings have more than kept pace with the rising cost of servicing the external debt. The fact that much of this debt is now in the form of equity holdings rather than fixed-interest obligations is a further element of strength, for dividends on equity investments can be remitted only when dividends are earned. It would take a depression of the utmost severity, accompanied by a catastrophic drop in export earnings, to raise the ratios to levels comparable to those reached in the 1920's and 1930's.

The size of Canada's annual foreign borrowings and the cumulative growth of the stock of foreign capital in Canada have not gone uncriticized. Anxieties have been expressed about Canada's ability to service her foreign debt should a serious depression develop. The very large deficit on current account that accompanies heavy capital imports has caused concern, some of it based on misunderstanding. The premium on the Canadian dollar, likewise a consequence of foreign borrowings, has handicapped Canadian exporters and the tourist trade. And there have been warnings from responsible public servants about the dangers involved in gearing the rate of economic development in Canada to a capital inflow that may not be sustained. Underlying many of the criticisms has been a seldom explicitly stated feeling that a nation as rich and mature as Canada ought not to depend on foreign capital as heavily as she does, and, combined with this, a serious disquiet about the implications of growing foreign ownership and control. To analyze these and other less weighty criticisms of the inflow of foreign capital would, however, take us too far afield. Our purpose in this chapter has been merely to present the statistics, emphasizing what is indeed obvious: that American investment in Canada has been heavy, that it has been growing cumulatively since the beginning of the century, and that it has contributed substantially to the development of the Canadian economy. The implications of this transfer of capital for the integration of the two economies will be examined in the chapters that follow.

CHAPTER III

The United States and the New Staples

Canada as a nation has been one of the largest and most consistent borrowers known to economic history. Its present prosperity and its high standard of living reflect the fact that these borrowings have, for the most part, been put to productive use. Its continued ability to attract foreign capital demonstrates the confidence that foreign investors place in its economic future and its good record as a borrower in the past.

But Canada has borrowed more than capital. The statistics of capital inflows that we examined in the last chapter are important in themselves, but they are also important as an index of a more inclusive transfer — a transfer of ideas, organizations, and technology. This is particularly true of direct investments. Direct investments typically involve the extension into Canada of organizations based in other countries; these organizations establish themselves in Canada for purposes of their own and bring with them their own business practices, their own methods of production, their own skilled personnel, and very often their own market outlets. If all Canadian borrowings from other countries were to cease tomorrow, these direct investment organizations would continue to exist and function. Many of them, indeed, would continue to expand, financing their growth from retained earnings. And the corporate linkages that integrate them — and the sectors of the Canadian economy that they control — with organizations in other countries would still survive. Bonds floated in other countries can in due course be redeemed or repatriated, leaving behind them no vestige of foreign ownership. But direct investments have no necessary termination to their existence and there is no method by which they can be brought under domestic ownership and control unless the organizations concerned are compelled or choose to make their shares available to Canadians. On the one hand, therefore, direct investments have the undeniable advantage of bringing with them experience and skills which the recipient country may lack and assured markets which it may need; on the other hand, they involve a potentially permanent cession of ownership and control by the recipient country to foreign interests.

Direct investment has consistently been a substantial fraction of total foreign investment in Canada in recent years, and its relative importance has been increasing (Table 27). Among the more obvious consequences has been a significant and, to some observers, highly disturbing increase in the extent of foreign ownership and control. Direct investment by the United States has formed by far the largest part of foreign direct investment (almost 85 per cent of the total at the end of 1957); particular attention has therefore been paid to the rising trend of ownership and control by the United

TABLE 27

Foreign Long-Term Capital Invested in Canada, Direct and Portfolio

	1926		1955		1957	
Type	$ billions	Per cent	$ billions	Per cent	$ billions	Per cent
All countries						
Direct	1.8	30	7.7	57	10.1	68
Portfolio	4.0	66	5.1	38	6.5	37
Miscellaneous	0.3	4	0.6	5	0.9	5
Totals	6.0	100	13.5	100	17.5	100
United States						
Direct	1.4	44	6.5	63	8.5	64
Portfolio	1.7	53	3.4	33	4.3	33
Miscellaneous	0.1	3	0.4	4	0.5	3
Totals	3.2	100	10.3	100	13.3	100

Source. Irving Brecher and S. S. Riesman, *Canada–United States Economic Relations*, p. 91, Table 18; Dominion Bureau of Statistics, *Canadian Balance, 1958*, p. 56, Table VIII.

Note: Figures are rounded to the nearest tenth of a billion; component parts therefore do not necessarily add to totals.

States. In some sectors, this trend has already gone very far. Many sectors of manufacturing industry and most of the resource industries are in fact dominated by United States-controlled corporations and receive their financing mostly from United States sources. Other sectors — housing, agriculture, utilities, institutional services, and government — are still financed predominantly by Canadians.

The tendencies are illustrated by statistics of the relative importance of nonresident (and particularly United States) ownership in selected Canadian industries at different dates. In railroads and public utilities, Canadian ownership has increased; but in manufacturing, mining, and the oil industry, nonresident ownership has tended to grow steadily. Table 28 presents some of the estimates.

TABLE 28

Nonresident Ownership as a Percentage of Selected Canadian Industries, Selected Year Ends, 1926–57

Industry	1926	1951	1954	1957
Percentage owned by all nonresidents				
Manufacturing	38	45	47	50
Petroleum and natural gas	—	—	60	64
Mining and smelting	37	51	53	56
Railroads	55	50	35	30
Other utilities	32	17	14	15
Total of above industries and merchandising	37	31	32	35
Percentage owned by U.S. residents				
Manufacturing	30	37	37	39
Petroleum and natural gas	—	—	57	58
Mining and smelting	28	45	47	46
Railroads	15	18	15	11
Other utilities	23	15	12	12
Total of above industries and merchandising	19	24	25	27

Source. Dominion Bureau of Statistics, *Canadian Balance, 1958*, p. 60, Table XII, and supplement.

Note: Investments are valued at book value. Estimates for the petroleum and natural gas industry are not separately available for years prior to 1954, the components of the industry appearing, in earlier years, in other categories of investment.

If the emphasis is on control rather than ownership, the percentages tend to be higher in industries in which direct investment companies are active and smaller in industries in which the nonresident stake is mostly portfolio investment. This is precisely what would be expected: United States direct investment companies may include a minority Canadian interest, but for statistical purposes the entire investment is classified as under United States control. In 1957, for example, United States residents controlled 43 per cent of the capital invested in Canadian manufacturing, 71 per cent of the total in petroleum and natural gas, and 52 per cent of the total in mining and smelting. In Canadian railroads, on the other hand, only 2 per cent of the capital was under United States control, and in utilities only 4 per cent.

The resource industries and the more rapidly growing sectors of secondary manufacturing are the areas in which American direct investment companies are particularly active. Typically, too, they are the largest firms and dominate the industrial sector to which they belong. In petroleum and natural gas, there are Imperial Oil, British-American, Texaco, California Standard, and Hudson's Bay Oil and Gas; in mining, there are International Nickel, Falconbridge Nickel, Sherritt Gordon, Britannia Mining and Smelting, Hudson Bay Mining and Smelting, the Iron Ore Company of Canada, Steep Rock Iron Mines, and the Utah Company; in asbestos, there are Johns-Manville and Quebec Asbestos; in aluminum refining, the Aluminum Company of Canada and The Canadian-British Aluminium Company (the latter partly owned in the United Kingdom); in pulp and paper, there is the Canadian International Paper Company; North American Cyanamid and International Fertilizers are prominent in the chemical industry; Westinghouse, General Electric, and RCA Victor in electrical apparatus; International Harvester and the John Deere Company in agricultural implements; Dominion Rubber, Goodyear, Firestone, and Goodrich in rubber; General Motors, Ford, Chrysler, Studebaker, and American Motors in automobiles; and Dupont and Canadian Celanese in synthetic textiles. Only in primary iron and steel, primary textiles, and lead-zinc and copper-gold mining, do Canadian firms play a dominant role. In most of the other industries mentioned, Canadian concerns are to be found among the half-dozen largest — Consolidated Paper and Abitibi Power and Paper in newsprint, for example, Massey-Harris-Ferguson and Cockshutt in farm implements, and Consolidated Mining and Smelting in nonferrous metals — but the American interest is typically predominant. Among the 13 firms in the Canadian petroleum industry having individual investments over $25 million, Brecher and Riesman found that 95 per cent of the capital invested was controlled by nonresidents; in mining, smelting, and refining, 14 firms had individual investments exceeding $25 million, and of this group 75 per cent of the capital was in firms controlled outside Canada. Of the 55 Canadian manufacturing enterprises with investments over the same amount, 26 were controlled by nonresidents and these accounted for 57 per cent of the capital invested in this group.[1] In each case, American direct investment firms represented by far the largest share of foreign control.

Many of these direct investment firms have gone to some lengths to take on a Canadian personality and speak with a Canadian accent, although, if the variety of complaints about their behavior is any guide, much remains to be done in this direction. That they have contributed very greatly to the development of the Canadian economy is undeniable. In fact their contribution is, strictly speaking, immeasurable, for it has included not only the investment of very large volumes of capital but also more intangible benefits: greater economic diversification, new skills, new products, and new methods of production. They have served indeed as a highly efficient channel of communication between the two countries, transferring to Canada with a remarkably short time-lag (sometimes with none at all) a wide variety of innovations in technology and business methods and giving to the two economies a remarkably similar coloration. If, to the casual observer, everyday life in most parts of Canada seems very similar to life in the United States, with the same supermarkets, the same brand-name goods, and the same advertising methods, the activities of these direct investment companies and the examples they have set are largely responsible.

Yet, if direct investment has stimulated economic development in Canada, it is also true that it has stimulated development in particular ways and particular directions. The effect has been to exert strong pressures toward economic integration. In secondary manufacturing, Canada has come to seem merely a northward extension of the domestic American market — a market with certain distinctive characteristics that an intelligent sales manager recognizes and responds to, which can be served either by shipments from factories in the United States, or, if the tariff is a significant obstacle, by the purchase or establishment of branch plants in Canada. In the resource industries, the impact of American direct investment has been different: Here, Canada's role has come to be that of a convenient and secure source of raw materials and semimanufactured products for American industry. In both fields, direct investment has tended to make Canada not a mere addition to, but an integral part of, the American economy.

The cumulative increase of American direct investment in Canada is, of course, not the only significant factor working in this direction. Portfolio investment also adds its weight, not through ownership and control, but rather by encouraging Canadian corporations and governments to rely on the American capital market when Canadian savings appear inadequate for their needs. Thus, monetary policies in the two countries become inextricably linked together, since any move toward tighter money in Canada encourages large borrowers to turn to the United States. But it is in external trade that the signs of integration are most obvious.

Canada's exports have always been highly concentrated,

in two quite different senses: The bulk of export earnings
has arisen from the sale of a relatively small number of
commodities, and a relatively few countries have taken an
overwhelmingly large proportion of all goods exported.
One implication of this dual concentration has been
that, throughout its history, Canada's material prosperity
— indeed, its viability as a nation — has turned upon the
conditions under which a relatively small number of
commodities could be produced and marketed. At times,
indeed, this "relatively small number of commodities"
has in effect narrowed down to one: wheat, for instance,
in the early twentieth century; square timber at an earlier
period; and beaver fur from the foundation of New France
until 1821, when the North West Company of Montreal
disappeared from the scene. These few export commodities have determined the whole course of the Canadian
economic drama; their expansions and declines have set
the pace for the action and have divided one scene from
the next. They are the great staple trades which have
traditionally formed the central theme of Canadian economic history.

The Canadian economy of today is a much more complex organization than it was in earlier centuries, and the
stark simplicity of structure that made it possible for
historians to relate almost everything that happened to
the fortunes of fur, timber, or wheat is now a thing of the
past. Canada now has a large and technologically advanced manufacturing sector;[2] the growth of trade, of the
service industries, and of government has swelled the
"tertiary occupations" whose expansion some economists
have taken as the hallmark of economic advance; and the
marketing of certain of Canada's important exports, such
as wheat, is regulated and stabilized by national and international organizations. These developments have intro-

duced new sources of growth and stability into the Canadian economy. Yet it is still true that the pace of development in Canada is determined fundamentally by the exports that enable Canada to pay its way in the world. And among these exports the staple trades, particularly the new staples, the products of Canada's twentieth-century resource industries, hold pride of place.

Canada's external trade is, on a per capita basis, the highest of any country in the world. Exports are responsible for almost 15 per cent of the gross national product, and the varying fortunes of the export trade affect the lives of individual citizens much more directly and immediately than, for example, in the United States, where the corresponding ratio is only about 5 per cent. Dependence on sales in external markets always introduces a certain instability into a country's economic life, since export earnings are sensitive to changes in demand, in government policies, and in the competition of rival producers over which the exporting country can exercise little control. The marked geographic concentration of Canada's exports adds to these risks. In 1958, more than three-quarters of Canada's total external trade was with only two countries: the United States and the United Kingdom. The country which ranked third in the list of Canada's trading partners, the Federal Republic of Germany, accounted for less than 4 per cent of the total.[3]

Canada marketed in the United States in 1958 almost three-fifths (59.1 per cent) of all her exports. More than 60 per cent of these exports to the United States represented forest products and nonferrous metals. If to these are added iron ore and nonmetallic minerals, the proportion rises to 71.7 per cent; and if exports of agricultural and animal products are included, it becomes almost 85 per cent (Table 29). Of the remaining 15 per cent, the

TABLE 29

Canada: Domestic Exports to the United States, 1958

Group	Value ($ thousands)	Per cent of total exports to the United States
Wood, wood products, and paper	1,163,180	41.1
Nonferrous metals	600,294	21.2
Nonmetallic minerals	188,968	6.7
Iron ore	77,749	2.7
Subtotals	2,030,191	71.7
Agricultural and vegetable products	79,542	2.8
Animals and animal products	290,517	10.3
Subtotals	2,400,250	84.8
All other commodities	432,012	15.2
Totals	2,832,262	100.0

Source. Dominion Bureau of Statistics, *Foreign Trade, 1958*, p. 62, Table IX.

Note: Electrical apparatus, n.o.p., has been subtracted from the total for nonferrous metals and products as given in this source.

only substantial items are farm implements and chemical fertilizers, both of which, thanks to the American farm vote, enter the United States duty-free.[4] A clear picture emerges, and it is one of which Canadians are very conscious: The overwhelming bulk of Canada's exports to the United States is made up of primary or semifabricated products. More than 70 per cent of the total represents raw materials for United States industry.

Figures like these are familiar to every Canadian who reads his daily newspaper or listens to his political representatives. Familiar too are the facts that the resource industries which provide the bulk of Canada's exports to the United States are the industries that have shown the most remarkable increases in output in the postwar years, that have absorbed much of the inflow of United States capital, and that tend to be controlled by United States corporations. Apart from secondary manufacturing, which is almost entirely a matter of servicing the Canadian domestic market, United States direct investment capital has been placed predominantly in those sectors of the Canadian economy that generate exports to the United States. These sectors are the resource industries — the industries that produce Canada's new staples. The older staple trades were oriented toward Europe; the capital investment they required came largely from Europe. The new staples are oriented toward the United States and are financed largely by the United States.

As evidence of economic integration, investment statistics and trade statistics tell the same story. To some extent, indeed, they are opposite sides of the same coin, for many of Canada's exports to the United States — perhaps most of them — originate with the United States-controlled firms whose operations are partially reflected in the investment statistics. Both kinds of evidence are the statistical symptoms of a process of reciprocal adjustment that is tending to merge the two economies into a single continental network of exchange. This process is more obvious when seen from the Canadian point of view, because there the stakes are higher and the external pressures felt more strongly. But it would be a serious error to overlook the fact that the adjustments are reciprocal. Unlike Canada, the United States has so far found it possible to be complacent about its role in the continental partnership. It may not be possible to maintain this comfortable attitude indefinitely: Canada is already the United States' best customer and most important single source of supply; every addition to American investment in Canada, every increment to Canada's share of the American market for

raw materials increases the integration of the two economies and thereby the dependence of each on the other.

Proximity to the United States, the ease with which
factors of production can cross the border, the broad
similarity of the two cultures, and the complementarity
of their resource endowments — these factors alone would
inevitably encourage close relationships between the two
national economies. Indeed, throughout Canada's economic history, they have done so. If the pace of economic
integration seems to have quickened in recent years, it is
partly an illusion. Much of Canada's current concern over
what is thought of as economic absorption by the United
States reflects merely a belated recognition of tendencies
that have been operative for many years. But this is not
the whole story. Economic integration has in fact acquired a new impetus in the past quarter-century, and
for this, two historical circumstances have been primarily
responsible. The first is obvious: the relative decline of
Europe as a source of capital and as a market for Canada's
exports. The second factor will occupy most of our attention in this chapter: This is the rapid increase in the
American demand for Canadian industrial raw materials,
arising basically from the cumulative expansion of American industry but accentuated by the progressive depletion
of certain domestic sources of supply within the United
States and — a consideration of particular relevance to
Canada — by the hazards associated with resource development overseas.

The depletion of domestic reserves of certain important
raw materials has, as is well known, been the source of
much anxiety in the United States in the postwar period.
Accustomed, with some reason, to consider themselves the
most generously endowed industrial nation known to
history, Americans have been reluctant to accept the

transition to the status of a "have-not" nation with respect to some of the resources essential to modern industry and to national security. The fact itself is still denied in some quarters, with considerable vehemence. And indeed there is a great deal of nonsense talked about resource depletion. Certainly it is incorrect to say that the United States is "running out" of industrial raw materials. Some, such as tungsten and nickel, the United States has never possessed in significant quantities. Others, such as coal and magnesium, are still available from domestic sources in quantities and at costs comparable with any source of supply. Depletion, where it is evident, is specific, affecting particular resources and not others. It shows itself, not as a sudden and dramatic exhaustion of supplies, but more gradually, in a trend toward rising real costs of discovery and development, a shift to lower grades, a dwindling of reserves that are known but not yet exploited. It is relative, becoming evident not merely in an absolute shrinkage of known supplies but also in the inability of known supplies to support a progressively rising level of demand at constant real costs. And its symptoms can be temporarily obscured, by government subsidies and tax concessions to the resource industries or, what amounts to the same thing, by tariff and quota protection against the competition of lower-cost resources in other parts of the world. Depletion is, in the case of nonrenewable resources, the inevitable result of resource use. It may be offset by new discoveries; its economic consequences may be neutralized by economies in use or by a shift to substitute materials; but as an underlying tendency, it is always present.

There are at least two points of view from which resource depletion can be discussed: that of the world as a whole, and that of particular nations. Many misunderstandings have arisen from confusing the two. One may be reasonably concerned about the heavy drafts that modern industrialism is making on the resources of our planet; but most of the arguments about depletion and its opposite, conservation, are nationalistic in tone and revolve around the allegedly harmful consequences that a particular nation may suffer — to its prosperity or to its security — if the sources of raw materials within its own political boundaries become inadequate to support the demands made on them. The economic arguments are mostly fallacious: Natural resources are merely one form of capital, and a reduction in this one form is not the same as a reduction in the nation's total capital stock. The security arguments are more weighty. It is no coincidence that most of the measures taken by the United States in recent years to protect its resource industries, such as the import quotas on oil, zinc, and lead, have been publicly defended in terms of the requirements of national security.[5]

In some respects, the change in the United States raw material position has been remarkable. Signs of serious depletion have, in the case of certain resources, become unmistakable; the raw material requirements of the economy, swollen by the defense effort, by stock-piling, and by the avoidance of major depressions, have increased cumulatively; and important new sources of raw materials have been opened up in other parts of the world. The result has been a marked trend toward dependence on foreign sources of supply. Suggestive evidence is provided by the trends in exports and imports. Less than fifty years ago, the United States was self-sufficient in practically all the basic materials required by its industries and in some cases had a surplus for export. Today it absorbs between 35 and 40 per cent of all basic materials produced in non-communist countries.[6] In the decade 1901–10, the United

States had an export surplus in crude materials and in semimanufactured goods; by 1956, there was a net import balance in both categories. In the case of certain of the most important industrial raw materials, the increased reliance on foreign sources of supply has been dramatic (Table 30). The shift from self-sufficiency or an export

TABLE 30

Selected Industrial Raw Materials: Ratio of Net U.S. Imports to U.S. Supply, 1937–39 and 1956

(percentages)

Raw material	1937–39 (average)	1956
Aluminum	0	11.3
Bauxite	53.0	78.1
Petroleum	0	13.5
Iron ore	2.6	20.3
Copper	0	22.4
Wool, apparel	21.9	43.9
Lead	0.2	56.5
Zinc	6.3	57.8
Fluorspar, all grades	13.4	59.5
Tungsten	41.8	59.7
Manganese	—	82.7
Nickel	99.2	95.5

Source. Percy W. Bidwell, *Raw Materials*, Table 2, p. 5.

Note: Supply equals production plus imports minus exports. Scrap and other reclaimed material have been omitted. Ferrotungsten and ferromanganese are not included in tungsten and manganese.

surplus to a net import balance has not, of course, been universal. The United States still meets all its own requirements of coal, molybdenum, magnesium, phosphate, and potash. But for tin, nickel, manganese, chromite, asbestos, and mica, dependence on imports is virtually complete. Defense authorities in the United States have classified some sixty industrial materials as strategic and critical.

In the case of 38 of these, the ratio of imports to new supply in 1955 was more than 80 per cent.[7]

The problem to be explained is not why the United States now finds it necessary to import many of its raw materials, but rather why the change did not occur earlier. The rapid industrial expansion of the United States has made tremendous drafts on the resource endowment of the country; the consumption of almost all materials has been increasing at compound rates, while new domestic resources have been made available much more slowly. In the Paley Report, it was estimated that there is scarcely a metal or mineral fuel of which the quantity used in the United States since World War I does not exceed the total used throughout the whole world in all previous history.[8] Growing population, rising per capita consumption, and ever-increasing mechanization of production have placed a heavy strain on both nonrenewable and renewable resources, but more on the former than on the latter. The result has been predictable: rapid depletion of the richer and more accessible reserves, a shift to deeper and lower-grade deposits, a trend to rising costs accentuated by the need to compete with manufacturing and the service industries for labor and capital, and a shift to lower–cost sources of supply available in other countries. Were it not for the economies in the use of metals that technical ingenuity has made possible and the growing importance of scrap and recycled materials, the shift to foreign sources of supply would have begun earlier and proceeded further.

The situation has been made to order for propagandists and professional viewers-with-alarm, notably those with a vested interest in the protection of the United States domestic resource industries. It has implications, however, for strategic planning, for international diplomacy, and for trade and investment policy that must be taken seriously. The broader issues will be postponed for later discussion. On an elementary level, however, it perhaps needs to be re-emphasized that a shift to the status of a net importer of industrial raw materials does not in and of itself imply any prejudicial consequences whatsoever for the American standard of living or for the rate of development of the American economy. Problems of adjustment there may be — the relative decline of particular regions or particular occupations that find it difficult to meet the competition of foreign supply sources — but essentially the process represents a rational reallocation of resources. Considerations of military security excepted, neither common sense nor economics provides any grounds for supposing that the national interest of the United States would be better served by opposing the trend rather than accepting it. The issue about which one may reasonably be concerned is, indeed, whether misdirected government policies, by opposing the trend, may burden the American economy with higher real costs for its essential raw materials than are necessary.[9]

The United States is at present the world's largest industrial economy; by the same token, it is the world's largest consumer of industrial raw materials. Conceivably it could — by the "engineering out" of scarce materials, by the use of lower-grade resources, and by technological substitution — reduce its dependence on foreign sources of supply very substantially.[10] Such a strategy of economic isolationism could take the United States out of competition for the available supplies of raw materials and thus alleviate the pressure on other industrial countries; but it would also cause a sharp reduction in American exports, aggravate the difficulties of the underdeveloped countries, and do irreparable damage to international economic cooperation. It is not, in fact, a strategy that has much to commend it, as long as the United States has access to nonhostile sources of supply in other parts of the world; and it is not the strategy that the United States corporations which are the principal users of industrial raw materials have, in general, chosen to follow.

The alternative strategy is the search for sources of supply outside the United States which, financed by American capital and developed by American managerial and engineering skills, can be used to supplement and if necessary replace dwindling domestic resources. This is the process that has been responsible for most of United States investment in the Canadian resource industries, though Canada is by no means the only area affected. Its operation can be identified with some precision.

The Paley Report is generally taken to be the most thorough survey of American raw material requirements made in recent years.[11] Its forecasts of future requirements may be too low, based as they are on conservative estimates of population growth, but its identification of particular resources which, in terms of United States domestic reserves, are already, or are likely soon to become, in short supply may be accepted as reliable. Of the twenty-nine "key commodities" whose future availability was considered by the Commission,[12] Canada was specified as a probable major source of supply for twelve. These were: iron ore, nickel, tungsten, copper, lead, zinc, cadmium, bismuth, aluminum, titanium, fluorspar, and asbestos.[13] In the case of cobalt, Canada was considered to be an important supplementary source. The Commission did not explicitly consider Canada's future role as a source of forest products, nor was attention given to Canada as a future exporter of energy to the United States, except with reference to joint development of such hydroelectric resources as the Columbia River and the St. Lawrence. Uranium was not discussed in this context, but was briefly referred to in connection with future technological possibilities.[14] Nevertheless, despite the restricted connotation given to the phrase "key commodities," the vital role that Canadian resources were expected to play stands out clearly.

Between the pattern of resource development in Canada in the postwar years and the pattern implied by the forecasts of the Paley Report, there is an unmistakable correspondence. This is all the more remarkable in that the flow of United States capital into the Canadian resource industries has been free from any kind of over-all control or direction. The forward planning of United States corporations has resulted, and is resulting, in an allocation of resource investments that corresponds very closely to anticipated resource needs. In some cases, of course, the pressures to conform to the predicted pattern have been almost irresistible. The exhaustion of the richer iron ore deposits of the Lake Superior region had been anticipated for some time. The massive development of the Quebec-Labrador deposits in Canada by a syndicate of United States and Canadian corporations represented a rational adjustment to the imperatives of the situation, as did a somewhat similar development in Venezuela and the production of sintered and beneficiated ores in Michigan. Similarly, as long as techniques for producing synthetic asbestos fibers continue to elude American scientists, growth in United States requirements must be met largely from the output of Quebec mines. But the response has not always been as inevitable and obvious as this, and even when the necessity has been obvious it has involved basic changes in trading relationships and in the structure of the Canadian economy. Construction of the St. Lawrence Seaway, to take only the most obvious example, was essential to the exploitation of the Quebec-Labrador deposits; so was the building of the town of Sept Isles and the construction of a 357-mile railroad into the hinterland. Canada's new northern frontier is Canadian only in a geographic and political sense; economically, it is a frontier of United States resource investment. The emerging pattern of resource depletion in the United States is fundamental to an understanding of the forces working to integrate the two nations into a continental economic system.

To summarize: The dominant motive for American direct investment in the Canadian resource industries is the desire to secure access to raw materials that are either not available, or available only at higher real costs, in the United States. The process represents a movement of factors of production to a location where their productivity is higher; it is an attempt to prevent rising real costs of production in the home country. It is important to note that the working-out of the process does not necessarily imply a stronger bargaining position for Canada, at least in the short run. In the first place, for the majority of the resources in question (nickel is an obvious exception), Canada is only one among several alternative sources of supply. Most industrial raw materials are available in a wide variety of locations; relative costs and the security of the investment are the dominant considerations in favoring one rather than the other. Because of proximity and other reasons, Canada has important comparative advantages as a supplier of United States industry, but in only a few exceptional cases are these advantages such as to confer any degree of monopoly power. Secondly, the mere fact that resources in Canada are being developed by United States interests does not necessarily carry with it unrestricted access to the United States market. There are typically established domestic producers within the United States who are in a position to exert effective political influence to protect their interests, particularly if they can plausibly argue that national security is involved. A higher level of costs in the domestic industry may prove, in this context, as much a political asset as it is an economic liability, for the charge of "unfair competition" from lower–cost foreign producers is one to which politicians are disposed to listen. Important regional interests within the United States may be involved, and these regional interests in many cases are the essential political support of key legislators.

✓ Many of these difficulties are, however, short-run in character. The United States tariff admits most industrial raw materials free or at nominal duties. Quotas and similar restrictions may be imposed at times of sagging prices and cyclically weakening demand, serving in this context as effective means of shifting most of the burden of adjustment on to foreign operations and foreign payrolls. Or the watchword of national security may be invoked, as recently in the case of petroleum, to maintain the level of earnings of the domestic industry. Nevertheless, the trend is clearly toward greater dependence on imports. Suggestive evidence is provided by the behavior of United States raw material imports during recent business cycles. Contractions in demand have, in a number of cases, been accompanied by cutbacks in domestic production that occur *before* cutbacks in imports. Sometimes, indeed, imports have increased while domestic production has been reduced. During the first few months of 1958, for instance, despite the fact that most of the cyclical decline was in the durable goods industries, United States imports of some of the major metals were unaffected. Imports of copper, lead, zinc, and iron ore were substantially higher than they had been a year earlier; and the decline in consumption was absorbed partly by a decline in domestic mine production, partly by rising inventories. Imports of metals which were not produced in the United States, and for which there was no "cushion" of domestic production, fell in consonance with the decline in demand.[15] R. A. Degen, in an investigation of American imports of newsprint, wood pulp, lumber, petroleum, iron ore, aluminum, copper, whisky, and zinc, reached similar conclusions.[16] Recent recessions have made little impression on imports of those commodities, imports of which were increasing relative to domestic production. The evidence is suggestive rather than positive, but the implication is clear: In those resource industries in which the United States is becoming increasingly dependent on foreign sources of supply, domestic rather than foreign producers are becoming the marginal suppliers.

Any discussion of these trends is complicated by questions of national security. Granted that in a world at peace it would be in the interests of the United States to draw its raw materials from the cheapest available source, is it prudent to follow the same precept today? Substantial material benefits may indeed follow unhindered trade in raw materials, but what if the price be military weakness? Defense, we are told on good authority, is more important than opulence. Stock-piling may offset to some extent the risk of loss of access to foreign sources of supply; but not all materials can be stock-piled, and no stock pile, however generous, can be the equivalent of an industry in being.

Considerations such as these have had their influence on public policy in the United States, not only in stock-piling authorizations but also in the so-called "defense amendment" to the Reciprocal Trade Agreements Act. Much of the emphasis laid on national security in this context stems from its acceptability as a cover for protectionist policies, the purpose of which is less the security of the nation than the subsidization of particular sectors of the economy. But this is merely the perversion of an entirely legitimate concern. Nothing could be more naive than to assume that policies admirably adapted to an environment of peaceful nations can be applied without modification to a world in which nuclear warfare — or aggression in more subtle forms — is an ever-present possibility.

Some of the more general implications of national security as it affects trade and investment policies will be examined in a later chapter. For the present, it is enough to point out that if American interest in Canadian resources would be predictable in a peaceful world, it is even more logical in the potentially explosive world of today. There are those who, impressed by the dangers of dependence on foreign sources of supply, are prepared to advocate a return to national economic self-sufficiency — the exclusive use, wherever possible, of resources located within the political boundaries of the United States. Most of those who have analyzed the situation, however, think in more continental terms. Serious strategic risk is seen in dependence on resources that must be transported to the United States by sea, over long distances, and from or through countries whose defensibility or political leanings are in doubt. But North American resources are, as it were, accorded a higher value in strategic terms. The distances over which they must be transferred are shorter; land transportation can be used instead of the high seas; and the countries of origin — that is, Canada and Mexico as well as the United States — are accepted as inevitably within the United States defense perimiter. In the Paley Report, for example, when the future availability of essential commodities was analyzed in terms of the strategic risks involved, a sharp distinction was made between requirements that could be fully met from North American (sometimes Western Hemisphere) sources and those that could not, and special types of government intervention were recommended to minimize the risks in the latter case. Edward S. Mason, one of the more level-headed students of the subject, assumes that the area that the United States must, at a minimum, consider itself committed to defend for strategic reasons includes North America, the Caribbean, and the northern half of South America; he argues that, if this space is controlled, the United States has no outside raw material interest to which substantial military resources need be diverted.[17]

For analytic purposes, it makes little difference whether we consider national security a relevant factor or not. The criteria for appraising the allocation of resource development expenditures remain comparative costs and the security of the investment. The term "costs," however, must be interpreted as including not only the money costs that appear in corporate bookkeeping, but also the extent to which military forces must be diverted from other strategic objectives to preserve access in time of war. And the security of the investment must be appraised not only in terms of risks of monetary loss, confiscation, or technological obsolescence, but also in terms of the risks involved in denial of access in periods of crisis. It requires no prolonged argument to demonstrate that, in the case of resources located in Canada, the diversion of resources required for their protection and the increment to strategic risk involved in depending on their use are negligible. To the extent that they enter into the calculation, therefore, considerations of military security reinforce the normal economic pressures toward continental integration.

There are cases in which the relevance of military security to resources policy is so clear that normal commercial considerations are completely overshadowed. It would hardly be prudent, for example, for the United States to rely on Communist China for its tungsten supplies, although the latter country has about 80 per cent of the world's reserves. From the corporate point of view, however, military security ordinarily appears as an additional complication in the already serious uncertainties involved in foreign resource development. These uncertainties have a direct influence upon the types of resource development that are undertaken, the locations that are selected, and the extent of the commitment that is made. The geographical distribution of United States direct foreign investment primarily reflects the presence of these uncertainties; military security has in most cases merely served to reinforce their influence.

Basic to an understanding of the problems involved in resource development in foreign countries is the fact that it involves the irrevocable commitment of massive volumes of capital for very long periods. Two factors are principally responsible for this. In the first place, for technological and geophysical reasons, almost all sources of industrial raw materials today require highly capital-intensive techniques for their efficient exploitation. Resource development has come to be almost exclusively a field for large organizations that are able to pour millions of dollars into a project with little expectation of immediate return. Such organizations must have financial resources large enough to enable them to wait and to accept the fact that, once the investment is made, it is likely to prove almost impossible to liquidate it. And they must have at their command managerial and scientific talent of a high order, competent to tackle problems that have never arisen before and devise acceptable solutions quickly. Typically, also, major resource development projects are located in areas that are sparsely populated, inadequately provided with power and transportation facilities, and lacking in the amenities that the work-force requires to maintain a reasonable standard of living. Consequently, the organization responsible finds itself involved in large allocations of capital for such purposes as the construction of railroads and highways, power plants, communication facilities, towns, and schools, which are indispensable to the execution of the project but yield little if any direct revenue. Thus, both the direct exploitation of the resource itself and the support of the facilities incidental to its exploitation demand an investment of capital which is large, not immediately remunerative, and almost irrevocable once made.

Adding its weight to these considerations is the fact that organizations competent to undertake resource developments of this nature are primarily interested in making available large volumes of raw materials over long periods. Economies of scale tend to make small projects inefficient; but, in addition, since the planning period is long, small projects cannot provide the quantities of output needed over the length of time involved. Thus a small-scale project not only tends to be high in cost for technological and organizational reasons, but it also does not meet the requirements of the corporation's planned supply schedule. The two factors reinforce each other, each pointing in the direction of massive investment and a long-period commitment.

Investments of this type inevitably involve a high degree of uncertainty: unpredicted difficulties in exploiting the resource; changes in prices, costs, and technology; and, particularly when the project is located in a foreign country, the risks of political harassment and punitive legislation. This is why major foreign resource developments are typically undertaken, not merely by large corporations, but frequently by syndicates of such corporations, pooling their financial resources and technical talents and minimizing the probable costs of failure for any single participant. Frequently, too, such cooperative arrangements provide some guarantee of stable markets for the product.

The degree of uncertainty that any private corporation or syndicate can undertake to handle is, however, limited, particularly in view of the fact that many of the critical variables are political in nature. Much of the contemporary emphasis on intergovernmental capital transfers — a striking contrast with nineteenth-century experience — arises from this fact. Only the largest and most powerful organizations, that is, national states, can reduce the uncertainties to manageable proportions, either by accepting direct responsibility for the mobilization and allocation of capital or by intervening indirectly to reduce the risks for private organizations. Most of the export of capital from the United States since the end of World War II has in fact been governmental, not private. This reflects partly the fact that the objectives sought, as for instance in postwar loans and grants for European reconstruction, have been primarily political. But it also reflects the very limited ability of private organizations to handle the uncertainties involved in international lending in the contemporary world and a rational appreciation on the part of private lenders of the risks to which international transfers of capital are now subject. This is particularly obvious in the case of capital transfers to the so-called

underdeveloped areas, a field in which private capital has
played a very minor role. The outflow of private capital
from the United States in 1956 and 1957 averaged
US$4.3 billion annually, but of this only some US$600
million went to the underdeveloped areas. The United
States government, in contrast, has been expending annually some US$2 billion in foreign aid and loans beyond
its direct arms shipments to its allies, and most of this
has gone to the less-developed areas.[18] Investment in
basic resource development in other countries is essential
if the future raw material requirements of the United
States are to be met. But so far private investment has
proved inadequate for the task. United States private
foreign investment has tended to concentrate in those
areas of the world that offer a relatively high degree of
security, principally Canada, Western Europe, and certain parts of Latin America.

Obstacles to the expansion of investment in resource
development are, in many parts of the world, serious
indeed.[19] Many of the less-developed countries have a
deep-seated antipathy to raw materials development,
associating it with foreign domination and economic
instability. Governments of formerly colonial areas, which
for the first time have taken their economic development
into their own hands, believe that the increase in real
incomes and national stature they so urgently desire is
to be achieved by rapid and diversified industrialization,
not by raw material production. The depression of the
1930's has left a profound distrust of raw materials as
a basis for economic progress: Continuous advance is
believed to be impossible for economies based on the
export of a few price-sensitive materials and vulnerable
to sharp falls in income, foreign exchange earnings, and
government revenues in periods of recession. And there

is concern lest, over the long run, the terms of trade of raw material producers will deteriorate, the prices of their exports falling relative to the price of manufactured goods. Beyond these factors, the ideology of nationalism and anticolonialism inspires demands for national owner- ship and national participation in management, pressures for financial arrangements disadvantageous to the foreign investors, and, what is equally a deterrent, fears of "creeping expropriation" as bargains originally entered into in good faith are progressively modified under the threat of punitive political action. Limitations on the convertibility of earnings, arbitrary administration of export and import controls, and legal uncertainties re- garding the status of alien property owners also serve to increase the hazards. And over all there frequently hangs the investor's lack of confidence in the political stability of the country to which his capital is committed.

Measures to reduce these hazards have been frequently discussed and in some cases implemented. Investment treaties and taxation agreements can provide some as- surance against arbitrary treatment. Tax concessions by the government of the investor's country and govern- mental guarantees against abnormal business risks may give some encouragement to the hesitant. Government loans, grants, and technical assistance for geological sur- veys, transportation improvements, harbors, power, and other basic services may reduce the outlays required from private interests and provide a more attractive eco- nomic environment. And international action to lessen the instability of raw material prices, supplemented by long-term purchase contracts and assurance against the imposition of tariffs and quotas, may reduce market un- certainties. But the fundamental sources of uncertainty — political instability and aggressive nationalism — remain untouched by measures like these. Long-run commitments of capital, of the type that resource development requires, are impossible without assurance that property rights shall be inviolate. This is the basic prerequisite; anything short of this is merely tinkering with the problem.

Foreign resource development, in the present state of world affairs, is inevitably a highly risky business. Government sponsorship can reduce the risks to some extent, but it cannot eliminate them. Conditions are propitious from the point of view of the investing corporation only if the foreign resource is unusually rich or indispensable and/or the foreign climate of investment unusually hospitable. The latter condition is likely to be met with only in countries that are relatively well advanced economically, politically stable, and culturally congruent with the United States. But rich and presently undeveloped resources are not common in such countries; the very fact that they have attained standards of living comparable with that of the United States is likely to mean that their resource endowments are known and are already being exploited. The unexploited but potentially rich resources of the world exist today, by and large, in areas that have been outside or on the margin of the spread of industrial, urban civilization. These are, to speak in general terms, the areas we call "underdeveloped." They are also the areas most affected at present by poverty, by the virus of anticolonialism, by suspicion of western capitalism, and by the deep-seated desire to become masters of their own political and economic destinies. Development of the natural resources of such countries by foreign corporations, particularly when the raw materials produced are destined for use outside the country of origin, is a delicate enterprise.

To these generalizations there are, fortunately, exceptions. And among the more significant exceptions are certain areas of the world which share approximately the same cultural traditions as the United States but which, for one reason or another, have industrialized more slowly and therefore have made more modest drafts on their resource endowments. These are the former "colonies of settlement" — parts of the earth's surface in which the original native populations, if any existed, were submerged by massive immigration from Europe and in which there developed cultures that were essentially variants of the western European model. These countries enjoy relatively high standards of living, largely because they have shared the technological and commercial biases characteristic of western civilization. Despite local variations, they are culturally similar to the United States, since they developed from the same European roots and underwent the same experience of frontier expansion. Politically, they share the belief in consent and antipathy to coercion that is the heritage of English liberalism. Economically, they are less highly industrialized than the United States or the western European nations, largely because their historical role, the basis for their past economic development, has been that of suppliers of raw materials to European markets.

Canada is not the only representative of this group, but, partly because of proximity and partly because of the nature of its resource endowment, it has felt the pull of American requirements earlier and more intensely than the others. To the extent that security of capital grows in importance in the geographical distribution of resource investment, trends already evident in Canada will be felt more strongly in other former colonies of settlement — Australia and New Zealand, for example

— as well as in the few remaining colonial areas where the imperial power still retains effective control. At present, however, Canada occupies a distinctive position as a field for American resource investment, for it offers at one and the same time all the advantages of a highly developed commercial society and all the attractions of a resource frontier whose potentialities have so far barely been tapped. The positive virtues of the developed and the undeveloped are there present in a single economy. A vigorous society, highly commercialized in its outlook, enjoying stable government under a well established political and legal system, alert to new opportunities for advance and yet conscious of its historical traditions, it can claim the second highest standard of living in the world and a climate for investment that, despite an embryonic nationalism, leaves little to be desired. At the same time, it commands resources of a richness and variety that were undreamed of fifty years ago and that, if they are to be developed efficiently, require exploitation on a large scale; they therefore must be sold in foreign as well as in domestic markets. Add to these considerations similarity of language and culture, geographical proximity, a closely integrated continental transport system, and commitment to joint defense, and the rationale for American investment in Canada becomes clear. So, indeed, does the nature of Canada's dilemma, for such close involvement brings penalties as well as benefits.

Some students of Canadian life with an eye for the ironic have suggested that, after slowly and painfully emerging from the status of a colony of Great Britain, the country is now developing into a kind of economic colony of the United States. It was, in fact, one of the most eminent of Canadian scholars who suggested that the

title of a popular history of Canada should be amended
to read "From Colony to Nation — to Colony." Such
manifestations of emergent Canadian nationalism at least
have the virtue of emphasizing indirectly one of the great
continuing themes of Canadian development — the country's historically demonstrated ability to improve its
standard of living, increase its population, extend its
boundaries, and integrate its widely separated regions
by producing raw materials for export. In this sense, the
twentieth-century realignment of the Canadian economy
toward the United States and away from Europe represents not novelty but an emphatic restatement of the
classic theme. As must be the case with every progressive
economy, Canada has developed by making appropriate
adjustments to opportunities. Errors of timing there have
been, of course — the overbuilding of the Canadian railroad system before World War I, for example; and there
have been periods, as for instance in the last quarter of
the nineteenth century, when opportunities seemed to
have disappeared. But in general, and over the long run,
the adjustments have been made and the opportunities
exploited.

In this context, the term "opportunity" implies a particular conjuncture of circumstances: the appearance of
a demand for a certain commodity; the application or
creation of a technology suitable for its production; the
availability or discovery within Canada of the necessary
physical resources; and the organization of capital, labor,
and managerial skills in such a way that the product can
be marketed and sold at a remunerative price. Many of
the products whose exploitation underlies Canada's current rate of economic development did not in earlier
years constitute "opportunities" in this sense. In some
cases, their presence was not known; more frequently,

even if known to be present, they were left undisturbed, either because high transport or production costs made their development unprofitable or because the necessary technology was not yet available. The existence of large iron ore deposits in the Quebec-Labrador region, for example, was known to Canadian geologists as early as 1893, but development did not begin until 1938 when the depletion of Lake Superior ores brought them within the margin of profitable exploitation. Many of Canada's most important deposits of nonferrous metals were known to exist for many years before they were profitably worked; technological advances, such as the introduction of the selective flotation process in the 1920's, have been essential for commercial development. Only rarely has the mere fact of discovery been sufficient to create economic opportunity in our sense. Changes in demand and changes in technology have, in Canada, created most of the opportunities for economic development.

The presence in Canada today of large resources of some of the most essential industrial raw materials results primarily from the fact that, in previous phases of the country's growth, these materials were not resources at all. Changes in technology and changes in demand were essential to make them so; earlier, they were merely "neutral stuff." The development of Canada in the eighteenth and nineteenth centuries was founded on other items — items that, in terms of the demands and technologies of the time, could be produced and sold at a profit. The beaver was not a resource until a change in European fashion brought beaver hats into demand. Canadian timber was not a resource until Great Britain, fearing loss of access to Baltic supplies, imposed a preferential tariff in favor of Canada. The soil of the prairies was not a resource until Marquis wheat, summer fallowing, transcontinental railroads, a fall in ocean freight rates, the chilled steel plough, and the roller flour mill made it possible for Canada to supply Europe with breadstuffs. And the industrial raw materials which Canada now exports to the United States were not resources until technological change made it possible to exploit them and the depletion of alternative sources of supply made it profitable to do so.

The fact that Canada is now in a position to supplement America's dwindling reserves of industrial raw materials is not, therefore, a mere accident of history and geology. The new industrialism of the twentieth century has vastly increased the demand for raw materials; but it has also increased and relocated the supply, by making resources out of what were not resources before. The pattern of Canada's earlier development, molded by geography, technology, and external demand, was not such as to make it then feasible or profitable to draw on the physical heritage that today has become so valued.

The transition from the old staples to the new has been analyzed in terms of a transition from European to North American markets and from European to North American financing. But it is also a transition in technology. The old staples were either luxuries (fur), or construction materials (timber), or basic foodstuffs (fish and wheat). They required no complex technology either for their production or for their use.[20] The new staples are industrial raw materials — metallic minerals, fuels, and newsprint — that, in the absence of a highly sophisticated technology, could be neither produced nor used. This, rather than the accidents of discovery, is the determining factor in the timing of their development. They are children of the new industrialism, the industrialism of mass literacy and mass urbanization, of electricity, the light metals, the alloy steels, and now nuclear power. Critical to their appearance in Canada has been the application of advanced technology, imported largely from the United States but also to a significant extent from Europe.

John H. Dales has suggested that the "Great Divide" in Canadian economic history between the old staples and the new may be dated by the introduction of hydroelectricity as a source of industrial energy, for which a convenient reference point might be the harnessing of Niagara Falls in 1895.[21] The advent of hydroelectricity, an innovation of critical importance for the newsprint and mining industries, without doubt marked the opening of a new phase in Canada's economic growth. For the first time, Canada, a country whose coal deposits are far distant from its centers of population, was provided with a potentially inexhaustible, though not unlimited, source of cheap energy. But the technological advances that ushered in the new staples went beyond hydroelectricity. The sulphite process, discovered in the United States and developed in Europe, was of major importance in the expansion of the newsprint industry and, in conjunction with hydroelectricity, relatively less-depleted forest resources, and governmental restrictions on the export of pulpwood, was a critical factor in the shift of newsprint production from the United States to Canada. In mining, the machine drill, the selective flotation process already referred to, the cyanidation process, and a wide variety of milling, hoisting, and excavating devices, most of them originating in the United States, were similarly crucial to the successful exploitation of Canada's ore deposits. In the case of aluminum and certain other metals, electrolytic smelting utilizing low-cost hydroelectricity has been the primary factor responsible for the establishment of the industry in Canada. The list could be extended almost indefinitely. Consider, for example, the change brought about in geological surveying by the advent of the airborne magnetometer and gravitometer, devices which have for the first time made possible the systematic surveying of very large areas and greatly reduced, though not eliminated, dependence on the clues provided by random outcroppings and the painfully won findings of the individual prospector. Consider, too, what techniques of airborne supply worked out in World War II have done to make possible the establishment of mining operations in areas remote from land transportation facilities. The greatest physical obstacle to Canada's development — distance — has been significantly reduced by techniques such as these; the scale of geography, as it were, has shrunk, and what was beyond the frontier of development in other days is now within it. The internal combustion engine makes mechanical power available in locations where human and animal energy would otherwise be the sole recourse; in addition, it makes it possible to move supplies in and move products out in areas that, in the days when the railroad and the steamboat were the only means of transporting bulk cargoes, would have been classed as inaccessible. And radio communication not only reduces the isolation that was in earlier times the inescapable concomitant of frontier development but also vastly increases the certainty, range, and rapidity of organizational control.

Technological changes such as these have altered the whole environment of opportunities for the Canadian economy, making possible effective responses to changes in demand that are themselves the result partly of technological advances in manufacturing, partly of the appearance of new products, and partly of the depletion of resources elsewhere. The opportunities so created have been opportunities not only for national development but also, on a different level, for private profit. In the absence of restrictions on the ownership of resources by foreigners, these opportunities have naturally attracted the attention both of Canadians and of entrepreneurs from other countries. Since the markets to be served are predominantly in the United States, and since the relevant innovations in technology have reached Canada in most cases from, or at least by way of, the United States, large-scale participation in the development of the new resources by American individuals and corporations has been inevitable. Reinforcing these factors are all the similarities of culture and institutions between the two countries that we have already stressed, and one important element in addition. Effective exploitation of these resources requires large organizations and large amounts of capital. Probably in time Canada could and would have supplied these on the scale required, without external aid. But American corporations and American entrepreneurial groups have typically been in a position to establish and finance the operations more quickly. Economies of scale in resource development have given a decided advantage to a country in which large pools of venture capital were already available and in which entrepreneurial groups, usually based on one or other of the great metropolitan centers, were already organized to mobilize facilities and direct strategy. Confident in the security of their investment, optimistic, usually with reason, of the richness of the resource and the long-run profitability of the market, such entrepreneurial groups have come to be the command centers that direct the advance of the resource frontier. Being already established, whether formally organized or not, they have been faced not with the unpredictable hazards of starting from scratch but rather with the calculated risks of extending operations into a new zone. International investment? Certainly it is, in a formal and statistical sense. More realistically, it is a geographical extension of the operations of established organizations. Entrepreneurship, skilled labor, organizational methods, advanced technology — all have been transferred. The transfer of capital serves merely as a convenient index of what has taken place.

What the pattern and rate of economic development in twentieth-century Canada would have been in the absence of this inflow of capital and skills from the United States is a question impossible to answer with certainty. Probably the rate of growth would have been slower; possibly it might have been more stable; beyond this, we can only speculate. If the inflow had been merely a permissive factor, making it possible to exploit opportunities for development a little more rapidly and a little more intensively, an assessment of its contribution might not be difficult. But more than this is involved. American capital, entrepreneurship, and technology have not merely exploited opportunities; they have also created them. Their function has been not merely to facilitate the doing of things that would have been done anyway, but also to get things done that might not have been done at all. They have been, in the true sense of that overworked word, dynamic factors in development. They have not only helped to accelerate the rate of development in the Canadian economy; they have also given that development a particular direction and quality, molding the structure of the economy into a form that reflects continental needs.

If the artificial stimuli of two world wars are left out of account, Canada has, in the twentieth century, experienced three periods of accelerated economic development: The first covers the years from 1900 to 1913; the second is the relatively short boom from 1920 to 1929; the third began in 1947 and, at the time of this writing, has not yet ended.

Each of these spurts of growth has had its own unique characteristics; yet all three have certain features in common, the principal feature being that the increase in capital formation that led to accelerated growth was in each case stimulated by an improvement in Canada's export trade. A mere rise in receipts from exports was not in itself sufficient; what was essential was confidence that export prospects were good and would remain so.[22] There has typically been a time-lag of several years between the rise in export earnings and the start of the investment boom. In the first period, for example, exports began climbing in 1896, but it was not until after 1900 that investment expenditures showed marked increases.[23] In the expansion of the 1920's, Canadian exports rose by more than 50 per cent between 1921 and 1925, but only after 1925 did the expansion, now stimulated by heavy investment spending, take on the proportions of a boom.[24] And similarly, in the most recent period, Canadian exports began to increase once again in 1947 after falling in the two previous years from their wartime peak; but the rate of growth of income remained fairly low until 1950, when investment expenditures began to rise very rapidly.

In each of these three periods, the export industries themselves have accounted for a relatively small proportion of the total capital expenditures that stimulated expansion. In the first period, prairie farm investment was 17.2 per cent of total investment in the years 1901–05 and 15.9 per cent from 1906 to 1910.[25] In the 1926–29 period, manufacturing and residential construction, which had no direct connection with export markets, accounted for the bulk of domestic investment, while the major export industries (agriculture, forestry, and mining) accounted for only some 15 per cent of the total.[26] The same pattern emerges in the period after World War II; mining, quarrying, oil wells, and forestry — the industries responsible for most of the surge in Canada's exports — accounted for only 5 per cent of Canadian gross domestic investment between 1947 and 1950 and only 7.6 per cent between 1953 and 1956. Finance, insurance, and real estate (which includes residential construction) accounted for 25.7 per cent in the first subperiod and 26.5 per cent in the second.[27]

If the importance of a particular sector to economic development were to be measured by the volume of expenditures for which it was directly responsible, we would have to conclude that it is on the industries oriented mainly to the domestic, not the export, market that Canada's development in the twentieth century has depended. And if we were interested merely in the growth of the size of the Canadian economy, there might be something to be said for this point of view. But if we are interested in causation, we must recognize that relatively minor changes in one sector can produce great effects elsewhere, and this is the case with the Canadian export industries. They employ directly a relatively small percentage of the labor force, and they account directly for a relatively small proportion of annual capital formation. Yet it is in the export industries that the growing points of the Canadian economy are to be found. Canada has never yet experienced a period of sustained economic development that was not based upon the expansion of one or more industries producing staples for export. This is partly because expansion in the export industries, if it is sustained, induces expansion elsewhere in the economy, leading finally to a volume of capital formation in other sectors (notably construction and transportation) that typically is much larger than that in the export industries themselves. Partly it is because the development of the export industries and the allied sectors attracts capital from other countries to supplement Canadian savings. And partly the effect is psychological: Rising exports and a belief that they will continue to rise encourage a mood of confidence and optimism that stimulates spending, both governmental and private, throughout the whole economy. It is as true today as it was in earlier centuries that the economic development of Canada turns on staple production for export.

The three periods of sustained peacetime expansion that Canada has experienced since 1900 have had different characteristics largely because the staples on which expansion has been based have been different. In particular, the role of foreign capital has been different. In the first period, from 1900 to 1913, the level of domestic capital formation was strongly affected by capital inflows; the same has been true of the expansion since 1947. In the 1920's, the relationship is much less clear: The level of investment in Canada rose steadily in this period, while inflows of capital fluctuated erratically. (See Chart I.) But the first and third periods, though they are more comparable with each other than they are with the intervening period, are also significantly different. Expansion from 1900 to 1913 was based upon the expansion of wheat exports to Europe, the settlement of the western prairies, and the industrialization and urbanization of central Canada. Capital imports were large and played an important part in sustaining the expansion; but relatively little of the foreign capital that entered Canada in this period was in the form of direct investment, and very little was invested in the export industry. Much of the inflow was absorbed by the transportation industry; manufacturing investment and construction took most of what was left. Prairie farm investment was financed almost entirely from the real savings of settlers and immigrants.[28]

The expansion which Canada has been experiencing since 1947, like its predecessors, has been based on staple production. There has been considerable growth in other sectors of the economy, but the pace of development has been set by autonomous investment in the resource industries. To this extent, the historic pattern of Canadian development is repeating itself. But there is a difference: The resource industries that produce Canada's new staples receive most of their financing from foreign sources. Many of them, as has been shown, are dominated by foreign corporations. In the 1900–13 period, foreign capital played a permissive, facilitating role; it was placed mostly, not in the export industry itself, but in sectors whose expansion was induced by the expansion of the export industry — transportation, construction, and manufacturing. In the period since World War II, on the other hand, the role of foreign capital has been much more autonomous; it has flowed largely into the export industries themselves. The induced investment in other sectors has been financed mostly from Canadian savings, though, to be sure, much foreign capital has also moved in to exploit profit opportunities in manufacturing.

Clearly, these are not black-and-white differences. It cannot be said, without qualification, that in the 1900–13 expansion autonomous investment in the staple industry came from domestic sources while in the current phase of development it has been financed by foreign capital. Much foreign capital that has entered Canada in the last fifteen years has been attracted by the profit opportunities inherent in a boom already well under way; much autonomous investment has been Canadian in origin. And it is hazardous to impute too close a connection between particular sources of finance capital and particular types of real capital formation. Nevertheless, the tendency is there, and it is of sufficient importance to be worth emphasizing. The autonomous investment that has furnished the impetus for Canada's current phase of accelerated development is much more closely linked to foreign sources of capital and foreign investment decisions than in any previous period of rapid expansion.[29]

Of critical importance in explaining this relationship is the role that American direct investment companies have come to play in the Canadian economy, particularly in the resource industries. This is a phenomenon that distinguishes the current period of expansion from its predecessors. It must be borne in mind that these corporations have at their disposal not only the transfers of funds from the United States, which appear in balance-of-payments statistics, but also their retained earnings and depreciation reserves. Their leverage in the economy is not to be measured by the annual estimates of direct investment inflows but rather by the total volume of investment funds that they control.[30] Nor is this all. These funds are typically reinvested in the most rapidly growing sectors of the Canadian economy, and their use is determined by organizations in a position to draw on extensive research and development facilities in the United States. Investment decisions made in such circumstances can have a catalytic quality that is not reflected in the dollar figures.

By any reasonable standard of comparison, the rate of economic development in postwar Canada has been satisfactory. There have been hesitations — real output did not increase at all in 1957 and 1958, for example — but the trend of growth, as measured by gross national expenditure in constant dollars, has been a creditable 3¾ per cent per year, or slightly higher than that of the United States.[31] What causes concern in Canada is not the rate of economic development (though some regard it as excessive) but rather its direction and its implications for Canada's future as an independent nation. Rapid economic development now seems to imply for Canada increasing economic integration with the United States. The new staples that provide the bulk of the country's export earnings are sent mostly to United States markets. The imports that these export earnings help to pay for come mostly from the same source. The foreign capital on which Canada relies to supplement her domestic savings is predominantly American in origin. In manufacturing and in the resource industries, large sectors of the economy are virtually dominated by subsidiaries of United States corporations. The insistence on rapid economic development and full employment makes the maintenance of a high rate of investment imperative and therefore reinforces the tendency toward integration. But even without this additional pressure, Canada's orientation toward United States markets and sources of supply would be extreme. Rapid economic development is urgently desired, but to the extent that it is achieved it carries with it consequences that are not desired. Exploitation of the opportunities for economic development that are evident in Canada has come to imply, in the mid-twentieth century, integration into a continental economic system dominated by the United States.

CHAPTER IV

The Canadian Reaction

It has always been difficult to generalize about Canada. What is true of one region is not true of another. Institutions, customs, and traditions that are characteristic of one sector of the population are regarded by others as strange and undesirable. There is an internal complexity and differentiation unusual in a country of barely 18 million inhabitants, and any observer who ascribes a single set of attitudes to the country as a whole can hardly avoid gross error.

Nevertheless, there has emerged in Canada in recent years a distinctive attitude to the United States — more strongly felt, to be sure, in some parts of the country and some sections of the community than in others, but general in its incidence and expression. Concern, uneasiness, suspicion, resentment, or hostility — whatever term is applied, it is encountered everywhere, and no visitor from the United States can be completely unaware of it. Its origins on the surface appear to be mainly economic, but no very profound analysis is required to show that the true sources of discontent lie at a deeper level. Bruce Hutchison has put the issue concisely. "The Canadian people," he writes, "are concerned with the specific, calculable frictions between the two neighboring states only as they touch on a non-specific, incalculable and seldom articulated thing which, for lack of a better word, we call Canadianism. Can a nation like ours, absolutely dependent upon its neighbor for defence, for markets and for capital, long endure? That is the real question on Canada's mind today, though seldom on its inarticulate tongue." [1]

The basis of Canadian anxieties is the conflict between two national aspirations: the desire for rapid economic development and the desire for cultural and political autonomy. There is nothing novel about either of these desires; each of them is characteristic of all cultures that have stemmed from the western European root. Together, they have underlain all the past history of Canada, and of the United States also. What is relatively novel about the contemporary situation is that Canada now finds itself so placed that the two aspirations are in conflict. Rapid economic development can be achieved only at the cost of a surrender, or what is felt to be a surrender, of some degree of autonomy. This conflict comes to its sharpest focus in connection with United States investment, since it is the inflow of United States capital that provides much of the impetus for Canada's current development, while it is in dependence on United States policies and United States-controlled corporations that the greatest threat to autonomy is seen.

No one doubts that American investment has accelerated the pace of economic development in Canada;

with minor exceptions, this is regarded as a positive good. Concern has focused partly on the degree of foreign ownership and control involved, but partly also on the implications for the direction and nature of Canadian development, as distinct from the rate. United States investment in Canadian resources has created a new frontier of development in Canada; but it also seems likely to convert Canada into a hinterland of United States industry. The two sources of concern come together in allegations that the contemporary pattern of resource-based growth is "unbalanced" and "financed by the sale of control over this country's productive resources to other nations." [2] Stronger expressions of the same sentiment could easily be found. Implicit here is a concern over the quality of growth as a matter separate from the rate, over the effects of foreign resource investment on the internal structure of the economy rather than on its total product. Growth that is based on an expansion of the primary producing sector is regarded as less desirable than growth accompanied by diversification and an expansion of the manufacturing sector.

Resource development in Canada in the twentieth century has, in the eyes of many Canadians, both positive and negative aspects. On the one hand, it has given new dimensions to the Canadian economy — new industries, new markets, new sources of income, and new potential for growth. It has provided the foundation for Canada's current prosperity and rate of economic expansion. It has improved, to some extent, the balance of economic power between regions, diminishing relatively the preponderance of southern Ontario and Quebec. It has opened up areas of the country, particularly in the north, that previously were regarded as inaccessible or of little economic worth. It has, in short, made Canada a larger, richer, and more powerful nation. In all these things, Canadians, with good reason, take pride. This is the positive side of the process.

On the other hand, twentieth-century resource development in Canada has implied closer dependence on United States markets and greater reliance on United States capital. In many of the resource industries, as in many sectors of secondary manufacturing, the largest and frequently the most enterprising firms are owned and controlled by foreigners. Further, production for the United States market carries with it vulnerability to United States trade policy. The power to create or destroy Canadian industries comes to lie in the hands of the United States Congress and Executive. Every step on the road toward economic development and a higher standard of living seems to be bought at the price of increased cession of control to foreigners, and each new project, each new victory over geography and climate comes to be tarnished by afterthoughts. To each spurt of expansion there is a corresponding shrinkage in Canada's freedom of action, in its self-reliance, and in its ability to chart its own course for the future. This is the negative side.

Certain facts are beyond dispute: The autonomous investment that supports Canada's current economic development is largely concentrated in the resource industries; much of the capital used in those industries comes from the United States; and most of the unmanufactured and partially manufactured materials that are produced by them are exported to United States markets. Does this mean that the net effect of American investment is to hinder the diversification of the Canadian economy? Is there any basis here for reasonable concern on the part of Canadians?

Implicit in the view that the present pattern of economic growth in Canada is unbalanced and represents an undesirable tendency toward specialization in primary production is a comparison with other economies — presumably the United States in particular — that are held to be in some sense more mature or perhaps more self-sufficient. Whether it would be desirable for Canada to attempt to model its economy on that of the United States is a question seldom explicitly discussed. It is relevant to point out, however, that the manufacturing sector of the Canadian economy is already as large as that of the United States, if both are expressed in terms of their contributions to the respective gross national products. This does not mean that Canadian manufacturing industry can produce the full range of goods produced by its counterpart in the United States, or that its productivity is as high; relative factor prices in the two countries and the economies of scale that result from a larger market are important here.[3] It does warn us, however, against the fallacy involved in thinking of Canada's internal economic structure in terms of the structure of its exports. Canadian secondary manufacturing industry contributes to the export trade only to a minor degree; it is oriented primarily to the domestic market. This does not mean that it can be ignored in a discussion of diversification. The same is true to an even greater degree of the so-called "tertiary industries" — services, finance, transportation, and government — whose products by their very nature cannot be exported but whose expansion has frequently been taken as an index of diversification.

It is true that Canada's export trade shows a marked concentration on primary and semimanufactured products; it is not true that this distribution of exports reflects an absence of diversification in Canada's internal economy. The secondary manufacturing sector is large relative to the size of the economy; it is in most branches technologically advanced; it has over the last half-century slowly but steadily grown in the diversity of its products and in the share of the domestic market that it services. Between 1939 and 1955, its real output almost tripled, outdistancing by a wide margin the growth in gross national product, population, and other industries. Table 31 shows the dimensions of the expansion.

TABLE 31

*Percentage Increase in Gross Domestic Product,
Secondary Manufacturing and Other Sectors*

Sector	1939–46	1946–55	1939–55
Secondary manufacturing	81	40	154
Agriculture	−10	19	7
Resource industries	15	97	127
Primary manufacturing	58	48	134
All services	59	37	118

Source. D. H. Fullerton and H. A. Hampson, *Secondary Manufacturing*, p. 30, Table B.

Note: Secondary manufacturing, as defined in this source, is a narrower classification than the usual Dominion Bureau of Statistics category of "manufacturing." It excludes those types of manufacturing which involve relatively minor processing of domestic resources or the production of industrial materials from natural resources for sale mainly in export markets. Pulp and paper production, for example, and smelting and refining are not included. Minus sign denotes a relative decrease.

Expansion in the resource industries has not competed with or inhibited the growth of manufacturing; rather, it has facilitated it. The survey of American branch plants conducted by Marshall, Southard, and Taylor in 1936 supplied suggestive evidence of this process: Among the 112 companies contained in the sample, the "Canadian content" of output increased from 69 per cent in 1926 to 72 per cent in 1929 and 81 per cent in 1933 (and this despite the fact that lumber and newsprint companies, the Canadian content of whose output is 100 per cent, were excluded).[4] Similar evidence can be derived from the Dominion Bureau of Statistics study of the inter-industry flow of goods and services in 1949 (the so-called "input-output table"). On the basis of this study, Caves and Holton have made estimates of the Canadian content of output in seven segments of Canadian manufacturing which indicate clearly the integration (in terms of input-output relationships) of the manufacturing and raw material-producing sectors (Table 32).

TABLE 32

Canadian Content of Total Output in Canadian Manufacturing

Sector	Canadian content of total output (per cent)
Food, beverages, and tobacco	94
Clothing and household goods	84
Forest products	97
Metal products	89
Electrical apparatus and supplies	90
Mineral products	79
Miscellaneous manufacturing	93

Source. Richard E. Caves and Richard H. Holton, *Canadian Economy*, p. 68, calculated from Dominion Bureau of Statistics, *The Inter-Industry Flow of Goods and Services, Canada, 1949* (Ottawa, 1956), Table 1.

There are circumstances in which specialization in the production of raw materials for export may inhibit internal diversification and the growth of manufacturing. But the opposite effect is equally possible. The critical difference lies in the production functions of the raw material-producing sectors — their requirements for capital and labor.[5]

If there were any evidence that the expansion of Canada's new staple industries had resulted in significant shortages of capital or labor in the other sectors of the economy, particularly in manufacturing, there would be grounds for believing that the much desired diversification was being inhibited.[6] In fact, the evidence shows nothing of the kind.

It is characteristic of the new staples that they have highly capital-intensive production functions. Their labor requirements are frequently critical, in the sense that scarce and high-priced skills are involved, but labor costs are small as a proportion of total costs. As a consequence, their expansion entails, in the aggregate, an unimportant diversion of Canada's labor force from other sectors. The situation was different with the older staples. The expansion of wheat production, for example, required a tremendous influx of population into the western prairies and extensive settlement of a large land area. Had it not been for large-scale immigration, which increased the total labor force simultaneously with the growth in labor requirements, the development of this staple could hardly have taken place. The new staples, however, make no such massive demands on the labor force; their expansion requires neither large-scale settlement in new areas nor an increase in immigration. Canada's recent immigrants have been absorbed primarily in the labor-intensive sectors of the economy, particularly the service occupations and construction, not in the resource industries. The frontier of development that the new staples are creating is not a frontier of settlement; whatever difficulties the older sectors of the economy may have experienced in the post-war period, none of them can be blamed on a diversion of labor to the resource sector.

The same generalization holds true with regard to

capital requirements, but for different reasons. The resource industries require very large inputs of capital, and
there can be little doubt that, if their growth had been
geared to the capital available from domestic sources
only, either the pace of resource development would have
been much slower, or other sectors would have been hard-
pressed to meet their capital needs, or both. The influx
of funds from the United States has, however, minimized
the problem, making it possible for the Canadian economy,
and particularly the resource sector, to maintain a rate of
growth much higher than could be supported by domestic
savings alone. Developments in the resource industries, to
the extent that they are financed by direct nonresident
investment, involve no drafts on domestic capital supplies
in Canada and consequently no diversion of capital from
other sectors. Indirectly, of course, some reallocation of
domestic capital supplies is highly probable, if not for
direct resource investment, then indirectly for the expansion of associated transportation systems, public services,
and ancillary industries. But of all conceivable methods of
financing resource development, the one least likely to
divert capital from other sectors is the one that has been
typical in the postwar period in Canada: direct investment
by foreign corporations and their subsidiaries.

The empirical evidence supports this conclusion. There
has emerged in the postwar period a particular distribution of investment funds in Canada, a kind of "division
of labor" by which Canadian capital flows mainly into
certain sectors of the economy and United States capital
into others. By and large, Canadian capital has concentrated on investment in agriculture, housing, merchandising, utilities, and governments. Much United States
capital also has gone into Canadian government securities
— 15½ per cent of all United States capital in Canada at

the end of 1957 was invested in government and munici-
pal bonds — but the greater part has represented equity
investment in the resource industries and certain sectors
of manufacturing. To put the matter crudely, Canadian
capital has shown a preference for the safer forms of
investment, that is, debt rather than equity, and the more
mature sectors of the economy rather than the newer
sectors. On the other hand, United States capital has
shown a preference for equity rather than debt, and for
the rapidly developing industries rather than the well
established sectors. To the extent that this is true, the
resource industries are not in direct competition with the
other sectors for capital; they draw on a qualitatively
different flow of funds and meet their financial needs from
other sources.

To explore the reasons for this distinctive channeling
of the investment flows would take us far afield. The
matter has been widely discussed in Canada, and it will
be sufficient for our present purposes to note that the most
obvious hypothesis, a psychological or cultural bias on
the part of Canadians against risk-taking ventures, is not
the only possible line of explanation and may not have
much to commend it. Certainly no less relevant are the
characteristics of the Canadian capital market: the fact
that a large proportion of total savings is generated by
corporations and therefore tends to be invested in lines
that carry on existing corporate activities; the limited
ability of the commercial banks, concerned as they must
be with liquidity, to supply long-term equity capital; the
preference of life insurance companies, pension funds,
and loan and trust companies for fixed-interest securities,
and so on. Also of importance is the fact that many Canadian industries are dominated by United States direct
investment companies, the majority of which do not make

their equity securities available for purchase by Canadians. The dominant consideration, however, at least as far as the resource industries are concerned, is probably the set of facts that we have already emphasized: the size and complexity of capital requirements in these industries; the need for advanced technology, specialized entrepreneurial skills, and some guarantee of assured markets; and the absence in Canada of organized entrepreneurial groups and large pools of venture capital comparable to those available in the United States. As Brecher and Riesman have pointed out, "what Canada has required . . . is an indivisible package of money, technology, skills and markets. It is this kind of package which non-residents have provided." [7]

Whichever line of explanation one prefers, the facts themselves remain clear: There has developed a rather sharp differentiation between those sectors of the Canadian economy that are financed predominantly by Canadian savings and those in which the rate of investment depends on the inflow of funds from the United States. The implications of this pattern are many, but our present purpose is merely to suggest that, in terms of capital supply, there is no evidence that developments in the resource industries have prejudiced the development of other sectors of the economy. What is true of capital is also true, as we have shown, of labor. It appears, therefore, that the expansion of the resource industries which underlies Canada's current economic development has not had the effect of inhibiting or retarding the diversification of the economy. In fact, quite the contrary appears to be the case. Investment in the resource industries has raised Canadian incomes and thus widened the market for Canadian manufactures. The products of the resource industries, though mostly exported in partially manufactured

form, have also served as inputs for secondary industry
and thus have served as a locational attraction for those
branches of secondary manufacturing (such as petro-
chemicals) that are most economically located near the
source of their raw materials. And in addition, the flow of
United States capital into the secondary manufacturing
sector, a flow normally smaller than that into the resource
industries but substantial nevertheless, has had the direct
effect of increasing diversification and counteracting any
tendencies toward extreme specialization in primary production.[8] Whatever may be true of other areas or other
periods in history, the capital-intensive resource development characteristic of present-day Canada serves not to
inhibit the internal diversification of the economy but
rather to encourage it.

There is no doubt that the phrase "hewers of wood and
drawers of water" should be added to the list of Great
Canadian Clichés[9] and barred from use in serious discussion thereafter. As a description of the internal structure of the Canadian economy, it is a mere caricature. The
Canadian economy is certainly undergoing marked struc-
tural change; but the change is in the direction of greater
differentiation, not greater simplicity. In one respect only
does the assertion of simplicity of structure make sense;
this is with respect to the export trade. As an international
trader, Canada lives by exporting the products of its
natural resource industries, since it is in these lines of
production that it has the greatest comparative advantage. This has been in the past the characteristic strategy
of Canadian development. It has been pursued, not as an
alternative to industrialization, but as a means of achieving and financing industrialization. It is still the strategy of
Canadian development today. Its success may be measured by Canada's continued ability to attract capital

imports, the continued expansion of its manufacturing sector, and the continued rise in its already high standard of living.

Concern over the direction or character of Canada's economic development must reduce, therefore, to concern over the costs that are involved in this pattern of dependence on staple exports, the term "costs" being interpreted in a sense that transcends the purely economic calculus. Certain of these costs are inherent in the situation of any country that specializes in international trade to the extent that Canada does: for example, the vulnerability to changes in demand and trade policy in other countries. This has been a recurrent theme throughout Canada's economic history, and it has lost none of its importance or urgency in the present day, despite the evolution of techniques for moderating business fluctuations and the partial steps that have been taken to limit arbitrary restrictions on international trade. Other costs, however, have their origin in Canada's particular situation vis-à-vis the United States, and it is in connection with these that most of Canada's present discontents have arisen.

The facts that the United States is Canada's best customer, that it is the supplier of most of Canada's imports and the source of most of its external capital, that the two economies are inextricably bound together by the imperatives of defense and the similarity of culture and language — all these are sometimes taken as grounds for satisfaction and mutual congratulation. By the same token, however, they are grounds for irritation and resentment, as the difficulties and conflicts of interest that are endemic in a world of sovereign nations come to be, for Canada, concentrated around its relations with the United States. It is the preponderance of the United States that causes the trouble. The same difficulties and conflicts, if diffused among a number of other nations, each exercising some influence on Canada's affairs and each restricting in some degree Canada's freedom of action, would hardly be worth attention. But Canada's situation is not of this type. In the course of following its own economic interests, it has found it both profitable and convenient to become ever more closely absorbed into a continental economic system in which the United States, by its very size and by its industrial and military power, must be the dominant partner. Resistances to external influence come, therefore, to be focused on the conflicts and disturbances for which the United States can be held responsible.

These conflicts are of many different varieties and range from the most particular to the most general. At one extreme, there are the petty excesses of officialdom: the shipment of Canadian ping-pong balls, for example, that were classified by the U.S. Customs — so the story went — as ammunition, because they could be used in pop-guns;[10] or the shipment of Chinese sesame seed which, when diverted from Vancouver to Seattle because of a shipping strike, could not be unloaded and forwarded to Canada because United States law prohibits trade with Communist China. At a different level, there are criticisms, not of specific acts, but of specific policies: the United States import restrictions on lead and zinc, for example; the impact on Canada's wheat exports of American surplus disposal programs; the attempts of the Department of Justice to apply the Sherman Act to Canadian corporations; the extension, for a time, to Canada of the oil import quota system; and so on. A whole series of resentments surrounds the policies, or what are supposed to be the policies, of United States-controlled corporations in Canada: their reluctance to employ Canadians in senior management positions; the tendency to centralize research in the American parent; the refusal to make it possible for Canadians to acquire an ownership interest in the Canadian subsidiaries; the subservience of the Canadian subsidiary to the export policies of the parent; the arbitrary setting of export prices when a Canadian firm sells only to its United States parent; the reluctance to participate in community relations and charitable drives to the extent that Canadian corporations do; and the virtual exclusion of Canadian enterprise from fields of manufacturing pre-empted by United States corporations. The absence of empirical support for most of these suppositions has not prevented many Canadians from believing them. And in each case what Congressmen Hays and Coffin, in their report to the Committee on Foreign Relations, termed "an attitude of bland indifference by the United States" has been as great an irritant as the acts and policies themselves.[11]

Most of these grievances, however, do not go to the root of the matter. They are symptoms of conflict only, and a disease is more than the sum of its symptoms. Canadians object, for instance, to the arbitrariness of United States trade policy; they resent any impediment placed in the way of Canada's exports to that country. But if all such arbitrary elements were removed, if the United States market were opened to Canadian exporters without let or hindrance, would the pressures toward continental integration be reduced? Would Canada then be more the master of its destiny, more at liberty to follow its own policies, or less exposed to the encroaching tide of American values and customs? Quite the contrary. Similarly, if all United States subsidiaries in Canada were to reform their ways and comport themselves in all respects as Canadians would wish them to, would the inflow of American capital cease? Would the Canadian economy become any

less dominated by United States firms? Again, quite the
contrary. Removal of the particular sources of contention
that currently attract attention would facilitate, not retard,
the very tendencies to which Canadians take exception.
The basic dilemma would remain: Canada's economic
interests, in present circumstances, impel it in the direction
of integration with the economy of the United States. If
this tendency to integration is to be resisted, it can only
be by sacrificing Canada's immediate economic interests.
Logically, those who oppose integration with the United
States should welcome, not criticize, every interference
with the flow of goods, capital, and ideas between the two
countries. Every move toward restrictionism in the United
States and every act of economic nationalism in that
country should be greeted as a boon to Canada. But
sentiment, not logic, is the arbiter of public opinion; it is
easier to be annoyed with the United States government
than with a historical process.

Ambivalence is, in fact, the leading characteristic of
the Canadian reaction. This reflects the dilemma in which
the country now finds itself and the transitional stage in
its economic alignments through which it is now passing.
Canada is at present going through a phase of growth in
which the economic orientation of the economy is decisively changing. Historically, the Canadian nation was
constructed along an east-west axis: From the days of
the fur trade onward, expansion took place by a series of
westward advances from an eastern base. All the older
staples, with the partial exception of the lumber trade,
reinforced this alignment. The Canadian transportation
system, the waterways and later the transcontinental
railroads, gave it physical expression. The protective tariff
helped to make it an economic reality by building up an
industrial sector in central Canada to serve the staple-

producing sectors elsewhere. The creation and maintenance of this simple, linear structure was, and to some extent still is, the primary economic responsibility of the Canadian federal government. Imports of capital from Britain helped to finance its building; and the export of staple products to Britain was its basic rationale. Any map of the Canadian transportation system illustrates the point; so does any map of Canada's population distribution. Immense though it is in total land area, economically and socially Canada *is* a series of narrow strips of inhabited territory joined together at the ends.

This historic linear structure is at present changing, and has been changing at least since World War I. The economy is going through a period of reorientation, as its traditional east-west axis, the basis of Confederation, becomes overlaid and intersected by a multiplicity of north-south connections. Canada's older staples, particularly the agricultural exports and some forest products, are still sent largely to the European market. The new staples, however, go mostly to the United States. The sources of Canada's imports show a similar shift: Nearly 70 per cent of Canada's imports now come from the United States and only a little over 10 per cent from Britain. The same pattern is evident in Canada's external borrowing: More than 80 per cent of all long-term foreign investment in recent years has originated in the United States as against some 15 per cent from Britain. Whatever economic indicator is used, the same conclusion emerges: a reorientation toward the United States and a relative decline of the older alignment toward Great Britain and Europe.

One is tempted to call the process inevitable, though this obscures the fact that reorientation toward the United States has been largely the result of Canada's pursuit of her own economic and strategic interests. It must be admitted, however, that many of the fundamental elements in the situation are not susceptible to change in the short run. The relative decline of Great Britain as a market and source of capital; the expansion of industrialism in the United States, with its consequent pressure on raw material supplies; the effects of technological change on the availability of Canadian resources — these are not the kind of thing that a shift in policy or a change in governments can do much to alter. And it must be remembered that the pressure toward continental integration experienced by Canada is not merely economic but is reinforced by other considerations: the exigencies of continental defense; the continuous exposure to American communications media; and the near impossibility of pursuing foreign policies significantly different from those of the United States. The situation is a confining one and the range of alternative strategies limited. In past history, Canada has been able to achieve certain of her own objectives by playing off one power against another — using the possibility of absorption by the United States to win concessions from Britain, and relying on the influence of Britain (sometimes with limited success) to win concessions from the United States. But the possibilities of this game are now largely exhausted. As far as Canada is concerned, the United Kingdom is now a relatively much smaller country and the United States a much larger one. Offsets to the influence of the United States are now slight. Ties of sentiment to Britain, of loyalty to the Crown, of membership in the Commonwealth are still important. For certain of Canada's exports, the remains of the imperial preferential tariff are still significant, though already eroded by inflation and now threatened by Britain's membership in a European free trade area. Investment in Canada by countries other than the United States has in recent years been increasing, though the aggregate is still insignificant compared with investment by the United States. Once these qualifications are made, however, there is not much more to be said. If Canada is to resist submergence by the United States, it must be almost entirely by her own efforts.

It is not easy to find a term appropriate to describe this process. Reorientation or realignment describe the change in economic structure and in trade and investment flows, but they are too narrow in their implications. Submergence, loss of independence, a dwindling of cultural autonomy are terms suggestive of what is involved but they lack precision. What is happening as a result of the realignment of Canada's economic relations is a gradual but cumulative narrowing of the range of alternative courses of action that Canada as a nation can choose to follow. There is no question of a loss of sovereignty in the formal sense, no immediate threat to Canada's national survival. Rather, what is feared and already experienced is a loss of identity, a gradual blurring-over of differences that are valued partly because they are differences. What Canada is experiencing now in its relations with the United States is, in fact, a threat to cultural survival rather similar to that which the French Canadians have been experiencing within Canada ever since 1760. It would be ironic if the strategies that the French Canadian community has so successfully used to insure the survival of its own sense of cultural integrity were now to prove adaptable to the needs of the English-speaking community.

Perhaps one of the most useful ways of describing what is happening is to say that Canada is becoming an economic and cultural satellite of the United States, meaning by this that its orbit, its path through time, is coming to be determined, partly by its own momentum, but partly also by the attraction of the larger and more massive economy to the south. The metaphor should at least remind us that a satellitic relationship to more powerful economies has been, for Canada, the historically normal state of affairs. Through most of Canada's history, its role was that of a satellite of Great Britain. The struggle for responsible government in Canada was a struggle against the more restrictive aspects of satellitic status; but long after responsible government was won, Canadians were generally content to think of their economic role as that of supplying the mother country with raw materials. The United States in this phase appeared as a threat to the British connection, a source of disturbance. Canadian national economic policy was a matter of resisting American encroachments; defensive expansionism was the principal means of defense, and integration across the continent along an east-west axis the dominant strategy.[12] Canada in this period, after flirting briefly with continental integration under the Reciprocity Treaty (1854-66), developed by exploiting to the full the opportunities inherent in a satellitic relationship with Great Britain. The gravitational pull of the American economy was felt continuously, most strongly when trade and investment ties between Canada and Britain appeared to be weakening, as after the repeal of the Corn Laws and the timber preferences. But Canada in this phase of its growth had room to maneuver. The competing pulls of the United States and Great Britain provided opportunities for channeling external pressures in directions congenial to Canadian goals. External control from Britain was patently dwindling as nineteenth-century liberalism encouraged the relaxation of imperial ties. External control from the United States was a threat which could be and was in fact countered by transcontinental expansion in Canada. Amid the interplay of pressures, there could emerge a characteristically Canadian strategy of development — one which promised both national expansion and increased freedom from external dominance.

If we wish to understand present-day Canadian sentiment, therefore, it is vital to bear in mind the fact that resistance to absorption or domination by the United States is the very essence of Canadian history. If there is any such thing as a Canadian nationality, it can be defined only in terms of the ways in which Canadians regard themselves as being different from Americans. This sense of difference goes back at least as far as the American Revolution; the Loyalist tradition is still strong in Ontario and the Maritimes, and not unknown elsewhere in Canada. The War of 1812, which most Americans think of as a squabble over the impressment of American seamen, is to Canadian schoolchildren a gallant and successful resistance to American invasion. Almost every exciting and dramatic episode in Canadian history — the Fenian raids of the 1840's, the Oregon boundary dispute, Confederation, the building of the Canadian Pacific Railway — is associated directly or indirectly with American expansionism and Canadian resistance. The times when Canada seemed to have lost its will to resist or to be relapsing into the grasp of the American republic — the Annexation Manifesto of 1849, for example, or the period of the Reciprocity Treaty — are thought of as regrettable deviations from the true path to nationhood. There is, of course, an element of myth in all this, but it is out of such myths, as Americans should know, that a tradition of nationalism is created. And even historians who pride themselves on their freedom from nationalistic bias must admit that the survival of Canada as a separate nation in North

America has in it something of the miraculous. An aggressive, self-confident republic, secure in its conviction that its manifest destiny points to continental empire, does not make the most comfortable of neighbors.

This tradition of resistance is still powerful at the present day, but scope for its expression in action is extremely limited. Economic interests point almost without exception toward integration with the United States, and a sense of tradition, of responsibility to generations of Canadians now dead and others still unborn, is a feeble defense against the lure of the dollar. The motives are unchanged, but the circumstances in which they must be translated into action are different. The question is whether Canada now has any room to maneuver, whether there exists any feasible strategy that can reasonably be expected to satisfy both the desire for economic development and the hunger for a separate identity. Such strategies have been found in the past, otherwise there would be no Canada today. Are they still available?

Concern over such questions is frequently expressed in terms of a demand for a "new National Policy." This is a phrase with special meaning to Canadians. The "National Policy" is the name given to what were in fact a number of interrelated policies adopted in the second half of the nineteenth century to create a transcontinental economy in Canada. Historians trace its origins to the period before Confederation, specifically to the adoption of Canada's first significant protective tariff in 1859.[13] Some are inclined to regard the confederation of the British provinces in North America in 1867 as itself part of the National Policy.[14] More commonly, however, the phrase is taken to refer to the program of railroad-building, industrialization, tariff protection, and western settlement inaugurated in the years after 1879. The main features of this program and the particular circumstances that made it possible are worth noting; they contrast significantly with what is possible and practicable today.

In the first place, the policy was a distinctively national one. It was adopted only after two other possible strategies of development had been abandoned: imperial economic integration with Great Britain and continental economic integration with the United States. Confidence in the first of these alternatives as a feasible basis for Canadian development was destroyed by the removal of British preferential tariffs in the 1840's and 1850's. Confidence in the second was lost when it became clear that the United States was determined not to renew the Reciprocity Treaty when its first term expired. With the disappearance of these alternatives, Canada was faced with the necessity of developing a national policy of its own, one based upon national, rather than continental or imperial, integration. Failing this, absorption by the United States, either by conquest or by annexation, was inevitable.

National economic integration in Canada was a feasible strategy for a number of reasons. The British North America Act of 1867 had created the political framework for a federal union which placed primary responsibility for development upon the central government. The new technology of the railroad made it possible to conceive of a transcontinental transport system that would channel goods, people, and ideas along an east-west axis, offsetting the north-south communications that the geography of the continent tended to encourage. The liquidation of the Hudson's Bay Company's proprietorship in Rupert's Land had placed in the hands of the federal government the vast resources of the western prairies, formerly the exclusive preserve of the fur trade and now a potential wheat-growing area of tremendous productivity. In central Canada, the area of greatest population density, the nuclei of manufacturing industry were already in existence; tariff protection and the markets created by settlement in the west could bring into existence in this area an industrial complex able to hold its own against the competition of American imports. If Canadian resources were inadequate for these tasks, British capital and British immigrants could be obtained to make their achievement possible.

This, then, was the National Policy, a program which, though carried through in the face of great difficulties, finally accomplished its purpose: the creation in North America of a viable transcontinental economy politically separate from the United States. Analytically, it can be described as a policy of defensive expansionism, a phrase suggestive of the two related objectives: defense against absorption by the United States and expansion in Canada. The point to be emphasized is that these two objectives reinforced each other; they did not conflict. Economic development in Canada was achieved by the same policies that strengthened defense against external control by the United States.

Is any analogous strategy available today? The choices that the country now faces are not totally different from those faced in the middle of the last century. Continental integration with the United States is no less a probability than it was then. Atlantic integration with Britain, perhaps in some more inclusive free trade area than is at present contemplated, is no less conceivable than in 1867, and no more. Is there a third alternative? More specifically, are there any feasible policies available to Canada today that promise both continued economic development and greater freedom from external control?

This question, expressed perhaps in slightly different terms, lies at the heart of contemporary Canadian political discussion. Around it cluster the major issues of policy that divide political parties today and that will shape the economic future of Canada tomorrow. It would be foolish, and perhaps impertinent, to offer a positive answer, because what is feasible and possible depends on what Canadians themselves choose to think of as feasible and possible, and in particular on the extent to which they are prepared to sacrifice certain of their goals in order to increase the likelihood of achieving others. It can be said with some confidence, however, that the difficulties involved in designing a new national policy are very much greater than those faced by the statesmen of the 1880's and 1890's. Indeed, quite apart from difficulties of implementation and execution, it is far from easy even to form an impression of what a new national policy would look like.

Consider the circumstances that made the first national policy possible. There then existed in western Canada a tremendous land area, untouched by any technology or mode of commerce save that of the fur trade, yet admirably adapted for large-scale agricultural settlement. This area, furthermore, with all its resources, was under the control of the federal government, which was accordingly in a position to set the terms under which settlement and development were to proceed, using the lure of free land to attract labor and capital. The form of staple production that this newly available hinterland could and did support — wheat cultivation — was such as to reinforce the east-west axis of Confederation and Canada's ties to Europe. The new technology of the railroad made it possible to supply this new staples area from an eastern base and to channel its production across the continent to eastern seaports. Capital for railroad construction came largely from Europe, and the additional labor force directly or indirectly from the same source. The entire process of settlement and development of the Canadian west served, indeed, to strengthen the east-west orientation of the Canadian economy and to counteract and partially neutralize the north-south pulls that earlier had seemed so formidable. Essential to the feasibility of the design were the availability of European capital and immigrants, the possession by the federal government of an immense public domain well suited to extensive agricultural settlement, and the availability of markets for the new staple in Europe.

Compare now the possibilities that exist today. Canada's new staples are marketed mostly in the United States. The frontier of development in Canada is no longer a frontier of settlement producing agricultural staples for Europe; it is a frontier of capital-intensive resource industries producing raw materials for the United States. Development, therefore, to the extent that it is based on these staples, must be in the direction of continental integration along north-south lines. This would still be true even if all the capital required for the development of these resource industries came from within Canada. In fact, however, the pull of the American market is reinforced by the corporate linkages that result from heavy dependence on American capital and technology. Furthermore, the resources on which these new staple industries are based are controlled by the provincial governments, not the federal government. National economic policy might conceivably point in the direction of a slower rate of resource development or a different system of resource priorities, but provincial governments respond to provincial needs and are little concerned to strengthen the east-west axis except where the old staples, such as wheat, are involved. There exists, in fact, no twentieth-century analogue to the process of prairie agricultural settlement under federal government control that played such a key role in nineteenth-century planning. Nor is there any counterpart to the technological revolution implicit in the construction of the transcontinental railroads. Most twentieth-century innovations in transportation — the aircraft, the automobile, and the truck (but not the pipeline)[15] — encourage radial patterns of development rather than the linear pattern that the old national policy exploited so effectively with the Canadian Pacific Railway. The tendencies inherent in the new staples — in the markets they serve, in their financing, and in the transport systems they utilize — run counter to the historic longitudinal axis around which the Canadian economy was built; increasingly, the burden of maintaining the traditional east-west axis falls on such federal responsibilities as the tariff and the regulation of railroad freight rates, converting these into chronic sources of federal-provincial conflict.

The first national policy was a feasible strategy of economic development by virtue of the particular conjuncture of opportunities in which it was designed and implemented: the existence of large unexploited resources under federal control; the availability of British investment capital; the ability to use agricultural settlement as a defense against American encroachment; and the effectiveness of railroads and a protective tariff as means of creating an east-west flow of traffic. Of fundamental importance were the characteristics of the staple itself: the high labor-intensity of wheat production and the fact that the export market lay in Europe. This combination of circumstances made possible a reconciliation of two objectives, economic expansion and greater national autonomy, which today, in a different conjuncture of opportunities, are incompatible. Long-run trends in technology, in resource development, and in the demand for industrial raw materials now make it in Canada's economic interests to accept increasingly close integration with the economy of the United States. These secular trends are harder to resist than military attack or aggressive annexationism. The threat they pose, if it is a threat, is a subtle one; its effectiveness lies in the fact that it is no longer in Canada's economic interests to resist. If there is to be resistance, its motives must be noneconomic, and it must be made at the cost of economic benefit.

Other long-run trends are also relevant. The national policy was implemented in a period when it was still possible for Canada to use Great Britain as a counterpoise to the influence of the United States. This is not possible in the same sense today. The construction of the Canadian Pacific Railway, the settlement of the prairies, the urbanization and industrialization of central Canada — these were tasks that, without external aid, Canada could not have accomplished at the time. But they were tasks undertaken at the high tide of British foreign investment, in a period when international trade and payments were free from the multiple restrictions that surround them today and when the risks inherent in international lending were much less formidable. Specifically, it was possible for Canada in that period to draw on Britain to supplement domestic sources of capital. Today, however, the United States, not Great Britain, is the major international investor, and it is to the United States that Canada looks for the capital needed to sustain its rate of growth. This is a situation not likely to be reversed within the foreseeable future. United States investment in Canada may level off or even decrease; Canada's economic develop-

ment may be restrained to a rate that domestic savings
can support unaided; but the massive inflows of capital
from Britain that made the execution of the national
policy possible will not be repeated. If Canadians choose
to maintain the rate of economic development that they
have now come to accept as normal, they must accept as
a consequence some degree of dependence on the United
States capital market. Whatever a new national policy
may involve in detail, it will certainly require heavy capital investment; it is hard to see how this can be attained
without increasing the very dependence on the United
States that such a policy would presumably be intended
to reduce.

These considerations are obvious enough. It requires
no sophisticated analysis to make their implications clear.
Why then is the demand for a new national policy still
heard? Partly, the demand reflects no more than a profound desire to escape from the dilemma in which Canada
now finds itself. The words still have a fine sound, no
matter how difficult it may be to attach any precise meaning to them. Partly, however, what is involved is a refusal to concede that the range of alternative possibilities
is as narrow as our argument up to this point might suggest. Still frequently encountered is a stubborn belief
that the future holds more for Canada than inexorable
integration into a continental economy. A deep-seated
desire for greater autonomy, combined with pride in the
nation's abilities and potential, induces a conviction that
there must be other alternatives.

That there are alternatives is not to be denied. What
is argued here is merely that these alternatives can be
followed only by a sacrifice of certain of Canada's immediate economic interests. This is not to assert that
these immediate economic interests will necessarily be

given priority over all other goals. Our purpose is not to predict what Canadians will choose to do, but merely to analyze what the alternative choices imply.

There is, however, at least one alternative strategy of development which has received considerable publicity in Canada but which turns out, when its implications are analyzed, to be really no alternative at all. We have already stressed the importance of western settlement in the first national policy. We have argued that there is no twentieth-century counterpart in Canada to this vast area of unexploited resources under federal control, and that, for this reason among others, a policy of defensive expansionism along lines analogous to the National Policy is not within the realm of feasibility.

But is not this argument based on a false premise? Is it not true that Canada still possesses a vast land area of unexploited resources, and that this area is under the control of the federal government, to be used for whatever national purposes that government may choose? What, in short, of the Canadian Northland — a huge public domain of potentially rich resources, as sparsely settled as were the prairies before the coming of the Canadian Pacific Railway, as little known in detail, but as exciting to the imagination and certainly no less pregnant with possibilities for Canada's economic future? Is it not true that an analysis of national policy in Canada that ignores the northern frontier is woefully incomplete, to say the least? Canada's first national policy was based on resource development in an area that had previously been the exclusive preserve of the hunter and trapper. Why cannot a new national policy be erected on similar foundations?

To meet this argument, it is not necessary to survey in detail what is known or suspected about the Canadian

Northland. On the basis of geological evidence, those who are in a position to know assure us that it is an area of great economic potential; they also assure us that it can never support extensive settlement. Agriculture may be possible for limited and local purposes in some parts of the Subarctic, which may be taken as extending north from the settled parts of all the provinces (except the Maritimes) to the tree-line. Where it does develop, however, it will be as an adjunct to settlement that takes place for the exploitation of other resources; it will not be a basis for growth in itself.[16] The pace and direction of economic development in the area will be determined essentially by the availability and marketability of its minerals — its uranium, zinc, lead, cobalt, nickel, and copper, its oil and gas, possibly its iron ore. At present, our knowledge of the mineral potential of the North is very limited; most of our estimates are deductions from the general geological characteristics of the area, supplemented by the very small amount of prospecting, drilling, and detailed surveying that has so far been done. But it is safe to say that it is on its mineral resources, supplemented by hydroelectric power, that the development of the area will be based.

If this is the case, certain implications are worth noting. Clearly the Canadian North will develop as a staple-producing region. The staples on which its future development must be based are identical with those currently produced by resource industries elsewhere in Canada. These resource industries are, as has been shown, oriented to the United States market, financed by United States capital, and frequently dominated by subsidiaries of United States firms. What reason is there to suppose that the process will work out in any different fashion as the frontier of resource development moves north? To be sure, supervision will lie with the federal government, not the provinces, and possibly this supervisory power may be exercised in such a way as to bring about a greater measure of Canadian participation than would otherwise occur.[17] The greater the urgency attached to northern development, however, the less important such restrictions are likely to prove. The basic considerations are those we have already stressed as affecting the resource industries as a whole: the need for large amounts of capital and large organizations and the overriding pull of the American market. It is futile, therefore, to expect northern resource development to result in any reduction of dependence on the United States. The more probable outcome is an increase. The northern frontier is a frontier of capital-intensive resource development, of large organizations and long-term investments. Difficulties of distance, terrain, and climate accentuate the uncertainties inherent in resource development, add to the costs, and increase the need for centralized direction and large financial reserves. The pattern of control and financing characteristic of the resource industries elsewhere in Canada is unlikely to be modified by a northward extension of the resource base.

From one point of view, the opening-up of the Canadian Northland in our time and the opening-up of the Canadian west in the 1880's and 1890's have much in common. Just as transcontinental expansion across the prairies created in Canada a sense of national purpose, a feeling that the country at last knew where it was going and why, so the concept of the new northern frontier has gripped the imagination of many Canadians today and led them to see in the north the image of a Canada richer, larger, and more powerful than in the past. By some mysterious dialectic, however, this belief in the

economic potential of the north has become identified
with aspirations for greater freedom from control and
influence by the United States.[18] In this respect, however,
northern expansion today and western expansion in the
late nineteenth century are totally dissimilar. Economically and strategically, the development of the Canadian
north is a reflection of continental needs; Canada's northern frontier is a resource frontier of North American
industrialism. Far from counteracting continental tendencies, northern development impresses them ever more
firmly on the structure of the Canadian economy. This is
an aspect of the matter that has not been emphasized
in Canada.

We are driven back, therefore, to our original line of
argument. Canada's fundamental problem is how to
create and maintain a separate nationality in North
America in the face of inextricable involvement — economic, political, strategic, and cultural — with the United
States. For a time in the late nineteenth century, a strategy
of development was found which held out the prospect
both of national economic expansion and of greater independence. No such strategy is available today. In contemporary circumstances, economic development and
greater national independence are conflicting goals:
Canada cannot have more of both simultaneously.

This is the basic dilemma of contemporary Canada.
Clearly, it constitutes a problem to which only Canadians
can find a solution, since it depends on a choice between
alternatives that only Canadians can make. Against the
background of this dilemma, the particular sources of
friction between the two countries can be seen in proper
perspective. The problem is not how to make United
States-controlled corporations in Canada behave like good
citizens; rather, it concerns what their presence and ac-

tivities mean for Canada even when they do behave like good citizens. Restrictions on Canadian trade with the United States may cause annoyance and resentment; but the more basic grounds for concern would still be present if no such restrictions existed. Underlying all particular manifestations of anti-American sentiment in Canada is a conflict that is purely Canadian. This is one reason why there has been so little understanding in other countries of the grounds for Canadian discontent: The conflict that is real to Canadians, a matter of immediate experience, can be grasped by non-Canadians only by intellectual effort. It is also one reason why Canadian political debate seems to follow much the same pattern no matter which of the two major parties is in power: The party in office defends certain policies because they are in Canada's economic interests, while the opposition attacks them because they tend toward greater integration with the United States. Conflict is an integral part of the situation. It is no uncommon experience to find on the front page of a Canadian newspaper one headline condemning Canada's dominance by United States industry and a second congratulating the United States administration for its adoption of a "continental approach" to the marketing of raw materials.

To criticize policies that interfere with the integration of the Canadian and American economies, and in the same breath condemn policies that promote integration, is hardly consistent in a logical sense. Yet ambivalence of this kind is common. For propaganda purposes, resentment against the United States can be aroused equally efficiently by either line of attack. What is resented in each case is not so much the policies involved, for their implications are seldom adequately analyzed, but rather the fact that decisions are being taken which have a profound effect on Canada's economic future but which Canadians themselves are usually powerless to influence. There is, in short, a feeling of helplessness, and in psychological terms this may well be the fundamental sentiment that underlies much of the current anxiety. The misdeeds of the United States are discussed in tedious detail; yet precisely what it is in Canada that is threatened by dependence on the United States is typically either left unexamined or else referred to in general terms such as sovereignty, independence, autonomy, or freedom. There is, of course, a reason for this: Canada's grievances against the United States are specific, easily identifiable, often expressible in the seemingly concrete terms of statistics; the things that are to be defended against the United States, on the other hand, are values and possibilities that can be discussed only as abstractions.

In recent years, under the ideological pressure of the cold war, Americans also have found it necessary to seek more precise definitions of the values and institutions that typify their way of life. So far, the search has produced little more than a rehash of familiar clichés. In the circumstances, therefore, comment on the difficulties Canadians have experienced in attempting to define the characteristics of Canadianism would be inappropriate. It should be pointed out, however, that this kind of self-evaluation is intrinsically more difficult for Canadians than for citizens of the United States. In the first place, Canada has two identifiable cultural traditions: that of the French-speaking community and that of the English-speaking sector. The former has been vigorously and effectively defended for two centuries, and it has a unity and integrity of its own. In the second place, Canadians, unlike Americans, are under the necessity of defining not merely a North American cultural pattern but also one that is different in significant respects from that of the United States. To emphasize merely the obvious differences between the culture of North America and those of Europe and Asia is, for Canadians, not enough. They must also identify the more subtle differentiations that mark them off from their neighbors to the south. And in the third place Canadians, unlike Americans, are exposed to a constant and unrelenting flood of cultural influences from a much larger continental partner. These influences, furthermore, are carried by mass media of communication which base their appeal on gross conformities in values and in so doing reinforce them, tending to submerge and obliterate local and regional differences.

It is far from clear, even to Canadians, what it is in Canada that is to be defended or protected from the United States. Is it perhaps political sovereignty? If survival as a separate nation, with its own political institutions and traditions, its own legal system, and its own party organizations, is what Canadians are primarily concerned to preserve, their anxieties are groundless, at least as far as any threat from the United States is involved. The days of annexationism are past. The reasons why this can be asserted with confidence are simple ones. It is not merely that the political absorption of Canada would be highly inconvenient for the United States, involving the danger of alienating public opinion in other countries and the certainty of upsetting the complicated coalitions and alignments of American domestic politics. The more weighty reason is that annexationism is unnecessary. The political absorption of Canada would advance no important American national interest; it is desired by no important pressure group; it is in no sense an objective to which the United States devotes any serious attention. What the United States wants from Canada it can already get without political unification. Such restrictions as exist on the transfer of raw materials are, in the aggregate, of minor importance and bear more heavily on Canada than on the United States. Access to the Canadian market can be secured, where the tariff would otherwise be a significant barrier, by direct investment in branch plants. Strategic bases have been made available, and the air defense of the continent is already under unified command. In foreign policy, the United States can normally count on Canadian support. Where policies have differed in tendency or emphasis, it has proved to the advantage of the United States that Canada should speak with a separate voice. Where they have not differed, the independent status of Canada's representatives has given their views a weight and significance that the United States has found useful. The political absorption of Canada is, from the point of view of the United States, undesirable and unnecessary. Joint membership in some larger federation, embracing other countries as well as Canada and the United States, is a possibility for the remote future; should it ever enter the realm of serious discussion, resistance to the sacrifice of sovereignty involved will certainly be much greater in the United States than in Canada.

In the nineteenth century, American expansionism was a real and ever-present threat to the survival of Canada as a separate political entity. It is not so today. The dynamics of expansion have changed as the industrial frontier has replaced the frontier of agrarian settlement. Twentieth-century industrialism exhibits, to be sure, a seemingly insatiable appetite for resources, but the land hunger of the nineteenth century, the impelling drive for territory that carried the American republic from the Appalachians to the Pacific, is now a thing of the past.

Access to industrial resources requires security of investment, respect for property rights, and freedom of trade; it does not necessarily require political sovereignty over the area of origin. Access to the land resources required to support a frontier of agrarian settlement, in contrast, required an enlargement of the area of political control.

But there is more to national independence than formal sovereignty. There is also the question of the range within which sovereignty can be exercised. Formal independence as a sovereign state may bring its own satisfactions, but it is a less vital matter, less likely to arouse sentiments of pride and allegiance, than the ability in fact to chart an independent course and follow it to its conclusion. What is at stake for Canada is not the ceremonial or formal aspects of its national sovereignty, but the efficient aspects. What is felt to be reduced and circumscribed is not the form of independence but its content. Internally and externally, the range of alternative courses of action which it is feasible for Canada to adopt becomes ever narrower as integration with the United States becomes more intimate. It is this shrinkage of the content of sovereignty that lies at the root of much Canadian discontent.

How much independence any sovereign state can enjoy today is a difficult question to answer. The division of the world into two armed camps, each organized around a continental power, offers few opportunities for autonomy in national policy. The shrinkage of alternatives that Canada is experiencing is not merely a Canadian problem, and it does not arise solely from proximity to the United States. The position of a middle power in the contemporary world is not an easy one, and possibilities for the exercise of an independent role are certain to remain very limited unless and until some disengagement from the two major power blocs becomes possible. Yet it would be idle to pretend that, even in a world at peace, Canada's fears of dominance by and submergence in the United States would be devoid of foundation. The erosion of effective sovereignty may be largely an unfortunate necessity of the cold war; but American influence on Canada has dimensions other than the political and economic.

If you ask a Canadian what it means to be a Canadian, he will answer you in terms of the ways in which Canadians feel themselves to be different from other nationalities; in particular, he will attempt to explain to you the respects in which Canadians are different from Americans. This feeling of difference is on a deeper level of analysis than the concern with sovereignty or national independence; it refers, implicitly or explicitly, to the distinctive characteristics of Canadian culture, particularly those characteristics that are held to be distinguishable from the culture of the United States. To specify what these distinctive characteristics are is no easy task; for our present purposes, the relevant consideration is that Canadians believe that they do exist and they set a value on them. It is true that economically Canada's prosperity and growth depend on ties with the United States. It is true that politically Canada now finds it extremely difficult to follow policies significantly different from those of the United States. These facts, however, are emotionally neutral except insofar as they involve, or are thought to involve, some diminution of the essential character of Canadianism. What is injured or threatened by these continental tendencies is, fundamentally, Canadians' image of themselves. It is only because this image, vague, imprecise, and hazy though it may be, is disturbed that emotions are aroused.

To list systematically the characteristic themes of Canadian culture would challenge the skills of the anthropologist and social psychologist; it is not a challenge to which Canadian intellectuals have so far made an effective response. It used to be held that Canadian culture could be differentiated from that of the United States by virtue of Canada's closer intellectual ties with Europe. There is, however, an element of myth in this belief. Both Canada and the United States have borrowed heavily from European culture; both are essentially variants of the same model. Compared with the United States, however, Canada has been but a marginal and passive participant in the trans-Atlantic exchange of ideas and values. "Between the United States and Europe," writes Frank Underhill, ". . . cultural exchange ever since 1783 has been a two-way traffic. Europe learned from America as well as America from Europe. Between us Canadians and Europe the cultural traffic has been almost entirely one-way. The more we boast of our special European ties, the clearer it becomes that we have remained colonial." [19] Whatever features of Canadian culture there may be that differentiate it from the United States, a more intimate involvement in the mainstreams of European thought is not among them. What then remains?

What remains is a possibility, the possibility that in time, as Canada matures and grows, she may develop a culture that is recognizably different from that of the United States, a distinctive phrasing of values that will enable Canadians to contribute positively to the variety and interest of human civilization rather than merely duplicating the attitudes and beliefs of their southern neighbors. The differences will surely never be very great; at the level of mass culture, it is very doubtful whether Canada can effectively resist the impact of American communications media. But the possibilities of significant differences of emphasis and interpretation at higher levels are still present. It is to preserve these possibilities of difference, rather than any manifest differences already existing, that Canadians feel compelled to resist absorption by the United States. What they seek to protect is a future potential rather than a present reality. The difficulties are great; but the objective is at least one to command respect.

CHAPTER V

Continental Integration and National Identity

Canada and the United States are already deeply involved in each other's affairs. If the analysis contained in the earlier chapters of this book is correct, tendencies exist which, if they persist, will make this involvement even closer. Predictions made on the assumption that present trends will continue are, however, notoriously unreliable. The process of continental integration will be hard to reverse; but this does not imply that policies aimed at retarding or halting it, or policies which, though aimed at other objectives, may incidentally retard or halt it, will not be adopted. In Canada, a serious attempt to check the movement toward integration with the United States is entirely conceivable. In the United States, the probability is rather that policies adopted for other reasons will impel Canada to adopt defensive or retaliatory measures.

It is necessary, therefore, to examine the implications for policy, in the United States and in Canada, of the processes we have been discussing. Continental integration can be accelerated or retarded. It can be accepted as a desirable goal or it can be resisted. Whichever way the choice is made in each country — acceptance or resistance, acceleration or retardation — what policies are available to implement the choice? And what policies adopted for other reasons are likely to have a significant influence?

Continental economic integration, carried to its logical conclusion, would involve the removal of all impediments to the transfer of goods, capital, labor, entrepreneurship, and technology between the two countries; it would entail the coordination of both internal and external economic policies; and it would require constant collaboration between governments on both sides of the border on all issues that affect their mutual interests. Both in Canada and in the United States, there exist significant elements of resistance to further movement in this direction. In Canada, the primary object of concern is the inflow of capital, with its implications for ownership and for the direction of economic growth, but trade issues are also highly significant. In the United States, investment issues are of minor importance; such concern as exists centers on trade policy.

Regarding Canada, we can be brief. All the factors we have mentioned as contributing to dissatisfaction with the growing influence of the United States are relevant here. Economic integration with the United States is regarded as diminishing the ability of Canadians to shape their own economic future. It is interpreted as tending toward an erosion of Canadian national sovereignty, a loss of independence in political and economic affairs, and a destruction of the possibility of evolving a distinctively Canadian way of life. Canada is seen as degenerating into the position of an economic colony, a vassal state. An emergent sense of nationalism induces an extreme sensitivity to United States policies and a profound resentment when Canadian interests are thought to be injured. Supported by, and supporting, sentiments of this kind are particular groups whose interests would be threatened by the reduction of trade barriers between Canada and the United States; others whose sales in foreign markets are injured by American competition; and still others who, identifying American influence with the influence of particular areas or interests in Canada, carry over their domestic antipathies into the international arena. Opposition to the spread of American influence is an essential raw material for Canadian political controversy and for the writers of newspaper editorials and lead articles. In politics and in the communications industry, there are many who, deprived of this resource, would find their occupation gone.

These sentiments have not so far had any decided influence on Canadian government policy, except insofar as they may have added force to Canada's protests against United States restrictions on trade or strengthened the determination of Canadian negotiators in dealing with the United States on issues of mutual concern. On most issues, the Canadian interest in reaching accommodation with the United States is so imperative that hostile sentiment has had to be ignored, verbally placated, or left to simmer until, at the next election, it can be brought to the boil for the political advantage of one party or the other. The situation is, however, unstable, reflecting as it does an uneasy equilibrium between the conflicting forces of nationalism and economic advantage. Under provocation, and with adroit management, it could become the dominant issue in Canadian politics and a more intransigent posture toward the United States might well result.

When we turn to the United States, the situation has an entirely different aspect. There is in the United States no hostility whatsoever toward Canada. The great majority of the population, in fact, seems hardly aware that Canada exists, except as an area on a map. The prevailing ignorance of Canadian affairs in the United States is, indeed, shocking. Much Canadian resentment can be traced to this one fact: To be pushed around by a muscular neighbor is upsetting, but to be pushed around by someone who is barely aware of your existence is an insult.

The principal reason why Americans have been and remain ignorant of Canada is that it has never been necessary for them to know very much. This situation is changing. Dependence is, after all, not wholly one way: A country that absorbs some 25 per cent of United States exports, that commands the now vulnerable northern frontier, that controls the land routes to Alaska, and that is the principal supplier of many essential raw materials is not to be taken for granted with impunity. The further regional economic integration proceeds in other parts of the world the more vital will relations with Canada become for the national interests of the United States. And there are indications that this is being recognized.

More recognition of this dependence-in-reverse, however, is not enough. Canada has few means of retaliating effectively against American policies that affect her adversely, and she has been reluctant to use those means she has. A weak bargaining position vis-à-vis the United States implies that mutual dependence, even when explicitly recognized by both parties, affords no guarantee that Canada's interests and aspirations will be given adequate recognition when United States policies are decided upon. There is no substitute, in this instance, for countervailing power. Lacking this, Canada in the past has been reduced to expressing her objections in terms of equity or fair play. Not surprisingly, the results have been disappointing. Experience has underlined a principle that could have been stated *a priori:* If Canada wants the United States to do something, she must be able to prove that it is in the national interests of the United States to do it.

Any distinction between domestic and foreign economic policies of the United States is, in this context, meaningless. The integration of the two economies has already proceeded so far that there is hardly any area of government economic policy in the United States that does not involve Canada to some degree. Lack of effective means of retaliation, and in particular lack of ability to exert effective pressure upon members of Congress, has meant, however, that in most cases it has been possible to ignore the Canadian interest. The only exceptions are cases in which it has been possible for Canada to associate her interests with the interests of particular groups in the United States who, for their own purposes, are prepared to support policies that Canada also supports. It was not Canada's long-repeated urgings that finally induced the United States Congress to approve participation in the building of the St. Lawrence Seaway, but rather New York State's need for hydroelectricity and the American steel industry's need for iron ore. Canada's protests against the American oil import quotas had less to do with the granting of an exemption to Canadian crude than the energy needs of the politically influential Pacific Coast states. Sales to American airlines of the CL-44, Canada's new air freighter, depend less on the price and quality of the aircraft than on the reluctance of the U.S. Treasury Department to sanction subsidies to the California aircraft industry. The pattern is a consistent one: Canada's involvement in United States policies is direct, but her ability to influence these policies is at best indirect.

It is easy to say that the national interest of the United States does not stop at the international boundary and that, in the complex weighing of means and ends that leads to the determination of national policy, Canadian interests ought to be considered despite Canada's limited ability to exert political pressure. This, however, is a normative judgment and takes insufficient account of the hard realities. The fact of the matter is that the weight given to Canadian interests in the determination of American national policy depends on the degree to which particular influential groups within the United States, in particular cases, regard their interests and Canada's as coinciding. If, therefore, we ask whether it is in the American national interest that economic integration with Canada should proceed further, we are in effect asking what groups within the United States would find their interests advanced by more intimate integration and what groups would regard themselves as likely to be injured. Operationally, this is the only meaning the question can have.

Let us then, for purposes of analysis, pose the question of continental integration directly. If the matter were raised now, as an issue on which a decision had to be taken, what would be the position of the United States? Let us suppose, purely hypothetically, that Canada were to propose to the United States the formation of a North American free trade area: Where would opposition be found in the United States and where support?

Much depends on circumstances. Confronted by regional trading blocs elsewhere in the world that gave evidence of a determination to restrict imports from other countries, the United States might well find the prospect of a similar regional free trade area in North America congenial. A less restrictive attitude in other areas would make purely bilateral tariff adjustments between the United States and Canada less attractive. As long as a multilateral approach to the removal of trade restrictions holds out reasonable prospects of advantage to the United States, interest in a purely North American free trade area is likely to be small. Should proposals for a North American free trade area ever enter the realm of practical discussion, however, opposition from certain sectors of the American economy is predictable.

First among these is undoubtedly agriculture. Unrestricted admission of Canadian farm products would render the American agricultural support programs unworkable, compel serious readjustments in farm prices and incomes, and greatly complicate an already complex American political issue. Here is a sector where the American and Canadian economies are still highly competitive. In both countries, agriculture is going through a period of very difficult adjustment and is heavily dependent on government aid. The removal of restrictions on trade in agricultural products between the two countries is, in present circumstances, politically impossible and is likely to remain so unless and until some degree of coordination of agricultural assistance programs in the two countries can be achieved, on a more rational basis, one may hope, than the programs currently in force. Any proposal for a North American free trade area would certainly be vigorously resisted by American agricultural interests. If one may judge by past history, this resistance would be politically effective. In order to have any reasonable prospect of acceptance, therefore, proposals for a free trade area in North America would either have to exclude trade in agricultural products completely, or else make separate provision for a very gradual reduction of trade restrictions on farm products in conjunction with an equally gradual coordination of price support programs. It is not without significance that the regional trading blocs now coming into existence in Europe have in a similar way and for similar reasons found it expedient to make separate provision for trade in agricultural products.

The second source of serious opposition in the United States to a North American free trade area would be the American resource industries, particularly those now dependent on tariff and quota protection to shield them from Canadian competition. The structure of the United States tariff, as is well known, tends to favor imports of materials in raw or semiprocessed form: The rates rise as the degree of fabrication increases. Abolition of duties and quotas would in some cases encourage a movement of refining and fabricating to Canada. It would also, however, deprive certain sectors of the American mineral industry of the protective devices that, in combination with government purchases for stock piles, have enabled them to remain in production despite a higher level of costs. Particularly sensitive are those sectors of the industry whose domestic resources have become seriously depleted. These are the groups that have been most active in recent years in seeking tariff and quota protection on grounds of national security. Zinc and lead are the chief examples; the petroleum industry until recently enjoyed protection from Canadian crude oil on similar grounds; pressure has also been applied for protection against imports of fluorspar, cobalt, and iron ore, but so far without success. In each case, the depletion of the domestic resource, implying increases in exploration, development, and production costs, has left the extractive industry in the United States highly vulnerable to import competition. Industrial consumers of these resources have been able to develop alternative and lower–cost sources of supply elsewhere, notably in Canada. But firms in the domestic producing industry have fought vigorously to remain in existence despite the availability of lower-cost imports. Implicit in the situation is a conflict of interest between two sectors of United States industry: the firms that have reacted to resource depletion by developing sources of supply outside the United States and those whose reaction has been to seek increased government protection for domestic supplies. In general, the domestic producers have been in a stronger position politically. Particularly in the Mountain states, their survival is of critical importance to the regional economy, and the organization of the United States Senate enables these regional interests to be very effectively represented. The "international" companies, on the other hand, have no similar regional base; such political influence as they possess tends to be exerted through the Executive departments rather than the Congress.

Such obstacles as have in recent years been placed in the way of the marketing of Canadian raw materials in the United States have arisen almost wholly from the political intervention of competing American raw material producers, many of whom would, in the absence of government protection, undoubtedly find it uneconomic to continue operating in their present locations. Were all artificial restrictions on raw material imports removed, many of the United States corporations involved might indeed find it possible and desirable to transfer their operations to lower–cost sources of supply in Canada; but serious injury to particular localities in the United States might nevertheless result. What is in the national interest is not necessarily in the interests of particular regions, and strong resistance to the elimination of trade barriers is therefore to be expected in state legislatures and in the Senate.

The so-called tertiary industries of the American economy (trade, finance, and transportation) can be passed over in this connection: They have little stake either in the promotion of continental integration or in resistance to it. There remains what is loosely called the manufacturing sector. Here it is very difficult to make any generalizations whatever. On the one hand, certain industries, including most producers of consumer durables, would have a strong interest in freer access to the Canadian market and little to fear from removal of restrictions on Canadian exports to the United States. Other industries, however, such as chemicals, automobiles, electrical apparatus, rubber goods, and synthetic textiles, have already adjusted to the existence of the Canadian tariff by the establishment of branch plants, and therefore they may have a vested interest in the maintenance of the tariff. It is not easy to estimate how serious this latter difficulty might prove. Certainly, it is fallacious to believe that the removal of tariff barriers would in itself offset the locational attractions of manufacturing within Canada, particularly when the investment has already been made. To hold that the removal of the tariff would result in the wholesale closing-down of American branch plants in Canada is to give the tariff more credit as a locational factor than it deserves. The more probable outcome would be a greater degree of specialization. Many American branch plants would continue to serve their regional markets in Canada. Others would specialize in particular product lines, selling both in Canada and in the United States, and reaping in the process the benefits of longer production runs than are at present possible. In particular cases, the fact of past investment in Canadian branch plants might moderate a corporation's interest in the elimination of the tariff; but, in general, opposition from American manufacturing industry would not be serious. Quite the contrary, in fact; if enthusiasm for free trade with Canada is to be expected anywhere in American industry, the secondary manufacturing sector is its most likely source. Unrestricted access to the Canadian market, together with the possibility of manufacturing in Canada for sale on both sides of the border, would be substantial inducements, particularly if circumstances were such that exports of American manufactures to other parts of the world were encountering difficulties.

It appears, therefore, that any proposal for complete free trade between the United States and Canada would encounter serious resistance from certain elements in the United States. On the assumption that trade in agricultural products could be excluded from the agreement, the most serious opposition would arise from the American mineral industry, particularly those sectors that are now dependent on trade restrictions to shield them from foreign competition. Whether this opposition could be overridden would depend primarily on the world trading environment. If regional trading blocs elsewhere in the world adopted exclusive or restrictive policies, the formation of a continental free trade area in North America would, from the point of view of the United States, appear an effective means of defense and retaliation. A less restrictive attitude on the part of trading blocs elsewhere, an attitude that left the door open for Canadian and American participation in some form, would render North American free trade politically and economically less attractive.

Canada's interest in United States trade policy is two-fold. The United States is Canada's principal customer and supplier; any shift toward protectionism has immediate and direct effects on Canada's trade. But in addition, United States policies do much to set the pattern for world trade in general; Canada, as the world's largest international trader, has an important interest in the repercussions of American policy on other countries. Today, as in the past, Canada's interest lies in the creation and maintenance of an unrestricted multilateral system of world trade and payments, a system in which she can sell her staple exports wherever the demand lies. Any merely regional system must be, for Canada, a second best, an expedient accepted only because other possibilities have failed. In particular, if Canada wishes to minimize the likelihood of absorption into a purely North American economy, it is in her interests to exert whatever political and economic influence she may have in the direction of a multilateral and nondiscriminatory reduction of United States tariff and quota restrictions, while at the same time keeping her own market open to the exports of the outside world. Any purely bilateral trade arrangements between the United States and Canada should be avoided, even though in the short run these may be to Canada's advantage.

These are precepts easily stated, but hard to apply. It is possible that Canada's trade with countries other than the United States may be damaged by the formation of regional free trade areas elsewhere. It appears unlikely at the moment that Canada's export trade will be seriously injured by the formation of the European Economic Community. In general terms, Canada's economy and that of the EEC members are complementary. The Free Trade Area, if it becomes a reality, will pose a more serious threat. Canada's exports to that market would face competition not only from the Scandinavian countries, with a pattern of comparative advantage very similar to Canada's, but also from British industry, and the possibility of a diversion of trade from Canada would be a real one.[1] To the extent that the formation of these and other regional blocs does result in damage to Canada's exports, pressures for bilateral trade arrangements between Canada and the United States will become severe. Bilateral tariff negotiations between the United States and Canada would open up potentials for reciprocal concessions that at present, when all concessions must be generalized through the most-favored-nation principle, cannot be explored. There has already been some discussion of these possibilities in Canada;[2] discrimination against Canada by the European blocs would undoubtedly encourage more serious consideration.

Preferential treatment for Canadian exports in the American market would probably be welcomed in Canada despite the fact that it would reinforce tendencies toward continental integration. To some extent, precedents for such preferential arrangements have already been set. Serious concern in the United States over the strategic vulnerability inherent in dependence on foreign sources of supply has in recent years been reflected in trade legislation. An incidental result has been the appearance of trading arrangements with Canada that are in effect bilateral and discriminatory. Canada's principal exports

to the United States are, as we have seen, industrial raw
materials, many of them produced in Canada by subsidiaries of United States corporations. The movement of
these raw materials to the industrial centers of the United
States is an intracontinental movement, using land transportation routes and inland waterways. To the extent that
strategic security of supply areas and transport routes is
regarded as a relevant consideration in trade policy, the
risk inherent in dependence on Canadian supplies is less
than that inherent in supplies imported from noncon-
tiguous areas over sea transport routes. Discrimination in
favor of Canadian supplies is, therefore, from the strategic
point of view, justifiable and necessary.

It is not necessary to evaluate this argument here.
What security of supply areas and transport routes means
in an age of nuclear warfare is not entirely clear; it could
be argued that the advent of long-range ballistic missiles
has made belief in the security of the heartland a trifle
old-fashioned. Be that as it may, security considerations
have in recent years come to play a significant, if not
yet a dominant, role in United States trade policy, and
the implications for Canada are of some importance.

Section 7 of the Trade Agreements Extension Act of
1955 (the so-called "defense amendment")[3] was passed
by Congress and accepted by the Executive as a compromise, a means of getting the Act extended without
including in it a long series of specific amendments excluding specific commodities from its provisions. It em-
powers the President to "adjust" the imports of any article
if he believes, after investigation, that it is being imported
"in such quantities as to threaten to impair the national
security." The vagueness of the wording was not ac-
cidental: Industries concerned over import competition
were given new grounds on which they might legitimately

demand protection, but the final decision was reserved for the Executive. Responsibility for conducting the necessary investigations, when protection against imports was sought, was delegated to the Office of Civil and Defense Mobilization. On this Office, therefore, was laid the not inconsiderable burden of deciding what national security meant in terms of material requirements and trade policy. The Act itself gave no guidance.

Potentially, it lay within the power of the OCDM to turn United States trade policies decisively in the direction of discrimination and protectionism; in fact, it still does. So far, however, the authority granted by the Act has been used with restraint. Applications for protection against imports under Section 7 have been received from a wide variety of industries, each of them prepared to demonstrate that they are vital to national security and that their survival is threatened by imports.[4] In only one case, however, that of crude oil and petroleum products, has the power to restrict imports on grounds of national security been used. And in this case, Canada has been exempted from the restrictions.

If any future American administration, rejecting trade liberalization as an objective, determines to turn the United States once again into a protectionist nation, it will find in the national security clause of the Reciprocal Trade Agreements Act all the statutory authority it can possibly need. What industry cannot make a reasonable case for its importance to national security? What industry, encountering competition from imports, cannot claim that its survival is being threatened? Actual injury need not be proved; a threat of injury is sufficient. For Canada in particular, the interpretation placed on this clause of the Act is a vital matter. The raw materials it exports to the United States fall, almost without exception, into the category of strategically essential commodities; most of them compete with domestic sources of supply in the United States. Does the national security of the United States require that American sources of supply be protected against Canadian competition? Or, in terms of national defense, are Canadian resources to be considered as equivalent to domestic supplies?

It may seem paradoxical that the United States, a nation which has undertaken by formal military alliance to guarantee the defense of its allies, not only in North America but also in Europe and the Middle and Far East, should restrict imports from those allies in the name of national security. A certain ambivalence of attitude may be suspected. More relevant to present purposes, however, is the fact that the introduction of security considerations into trade policy necessarily involves discrimination, *de facto* if not *de iure*, between different sources of supply. Since all sources of supply are not equally secure, all cannot be treated alike. To the extent that security is used as a justification for trade restrictions, discrimination becomes inevitable.

It appeared at one time as if the OCDM intended to interpret the material requirements of national security in terms of United States resources alone. More recently, however, a less nationalistic approach has been evident. The history of the oil import quotas illustrates the point. When restrictions on the importation of crude oil into the United States were first seriously proposed in 1953–54, both Canada and Venezuela were to be exempted from the scheme, on the grounds that imports from these countries did not involve the same strategic risks as did imports from the Middle and Far East. No restrictive measures were in fact taken at that time, largely because the Suez crisis intervened to relieve the pressure of Middle

East oil on United States domestic producers. In 1957, however, the question of import restrictions was again raised, this time in terms of the defense amendment to the Reciprocal Trade Act. In April of that year, the Office of Defense Mobilization (as OCDM was then called) declared that imports were in fact threatening the national security, and in June a "voluntary" system of import quotas was adopted by which the importing companies were themselves expected to restrict their purchases of foreign, including Canadian, crude by stipulated amounts. The failure of certain large importers to cooperate in this scheme, together with the growing pressure of imports from the Middle East, led to the imposition of mandatory restrictions in March 1959. These were applied to refined products as well as to crude oil, and to imports from Canada and Venezuela as well as from the Middle and Far East.

The security risk seen in the situation arose from the depressing effect of low-cost imports on drilling operations and the development of new oil reserves in the United States. The real threat came from the tremendous reserves of low-cost petroleum in the Middle East. Canada and Venezuela, where production costs were only slightly lower than in the United States, were involved only incidentally, but were nevertheless included in the restrictions. Neither in the report of the committee that proposed the scheme (the Special Committee to Investigate Crude Oil Imports) nor in the President's proclamation that directed it to be implemented was there any suggestion that Canadian oil might be, from the security point of view, in a different category from Middle East supplies. Imports were retarding the search for new oil reserves in the United States; it was vital to the security of the United States that new reserves should be discovered;

therefore, imports should be restricted. From this point of view, there were no grounds for discrimination.

There were already hints, however, that modifications might be made. The statement issued by the President on March 10, 1959, recognized that the United States had, in common with Canada and the American republics, "a joint interest in hemisphere defense." And at the end of April, after vigorous protests from the Canadian government, an exemption from the quota system was granted, not to Canada and Venezuela, but to oil entering the United States over land, by pipeline, truck or tank car. Thus was the semblance of nondiscrimination preserved. In effect, however, the restrictions were modified so as to discriminate in favor of Canada and Mexico.[5]

Not unnaturally, this kind of discrimination caused little heart-searching among Canadians, most of whom interpreted the exemption as evidence that the American authorities were willing to adopt a "continental approach" to raw material problems. Further evidence was provided by the findings of the OCDM with respect to fluorspar and cobalt. In each of these cases, investigations led to the conclusion that, although imports were indeed increasing, no threat to national security was involved. The reason given was that domestic producers were not the only source of supply on which the United States could count. In the case of fluorspar, it was estimated that reliance on domestic production alone would mean the complete exhaustion of the high-grade domestic reserves within eleven years, with little likelihood of important new discoveries being made. Mexico and Canada, however, had substantial reserves which would be available to the United States in the event of emergency. The significant issue was disposed of in these terms: "Since resources in Mexico and Canada are considered to be as accessible as domestic production, these reserves more than double our potential mobilization resources. . . . The geographical base for current mobilization supply under the most drastic mobilization conditions is North America." [6] A similar conclusion was reached with regard to cobalt. The principal foreign source of the metal was the Belgian Congo, an area of doubtful strategic security. But Canadian production had doubled since 1953, additional supplies were expected to be available from Cuba, the Bethlehem Steel Company in the United States was producing cobalt as a by-product of iron-ore mining in Pennsylvania, and the cobalt already on hand in United States government inventories was in excess of the maximum stock pile objective. In the circumstances, it could hardly be said that imports of cobalt were threatening to impair national security. [7]

What do these decisions imply for Canada? In the first place, they imply that Canadian resources are now considered to be equivalent to United States domestic resources in their relation to national security. Secondly, they imply that, should restriction of particular classes of imports be regarded as necessary to the security of the United States, Canada may reasonably expect exemption from the restrictive measures applied to the exports of other countries. The entry of security considerations into United States trade policy, in short, encourages purely bilateral arrangements between the United States and Canada and consequently discrimination against other sources of supply. If, as seems possible, such considerations in the future acquire increasing importance in United States trade policy, they will tend to bring into existence in North America, not indeed a free trade area, but a preferential trading system. [8] Preferential treatment for Canadian exports, granted on grounds of strategic security, will strongly reinforce the continental pressures already operating.

If Canada seriously wishes to resist or retard the process of continental economic integration, she should refuse to accept such discriminatory treatment when it is offered. It is, indeed, by Canada's reaction to such bilateral proposals that outside observers will be inclined to gauge what weight Canadians do in fact attach to their autonomy and what sacrifices of economic advantage they are prepared to make to achieve it. Certainly the Canadian reaction to the exemption of Canadian crude from the oil import quotas did not suggest a disposition to make common cause with other western hemisphere producers. Indeed Canadians, who have seen their air defense completely integrated with that of the United States, who have accepted the establishment of American missile bases on their own soil, and who are painfully aware that their retaliatory power in the event of attack depends on the use of nuclear devices which, by American law, must remain in American custody, are more inclined to regard the original imposition of quotas on Canadian crude oil as a hypocritical absurdity, and to demand that the treatment belatedly granted to this commodity be extended to their other exports also. If Canadian resources are in fact as secure as resources within the boundaries of the United States, why are import quotas still imposed on Canadian zinc and lead? If Canadian and American air defense is really one and indivisible, why are Canadian firms not permitted to bid on defense contracts on the same basis as American firms? If the Director of OCDM can state flatly that the geographical base for mobilization supply is North America, why is any distinction whatsoever made between Canadian and American raw materials?

This attitude is entirely understandable and must com-

mand sympathy. There is no doubt that a selective lower-
ing of trade barriers between the United States and Canada, whether discriminatory or not, would bring substantial economic benefits to both countries. And the application to Canada of the security argument for trade
restriction is nonsensical. Nevertheless, what is involved
here is merely one particular aspect of the much broader
issue to which we have already referred. Canada's economic interests impel her in the direction of continental
economic integration. If this process is to be halted or
retarded, it can be only by the sacrifice of economic advantage. Preferential access to the United States market
for raw materials may be a particularly difficult lure to
resist, but the preservation of a measure of economic
autonomy, if this is what Canadians want, can be achieved
only by hard choices of precisely this nature.

If Canada wishes to retard the processes that are tending to promote continental economic integration, policies
that will produce this result are certainly available. There
are more effective methods than the painful self-denial
involved in refusal to accept bilateral trade concessions.
The contemporary world is, after all, replete with il-
lustrations of what a nation should do if it does not wish to
attract private investment from the United States, if it
does not desire to encourage the development of its resources by American corporations, and if it has no interest
in promoting the sale of its exports in American markets.
All that is necessary is that Canada should follow the
examples that nationalistic sentiment elsewhere in the
world has provided so generously.

What is presumably required is some method of making
Canada a less attractive field for American investment.
Discriminatory taxation is an obvious possibility. Tech-
niques of insuring that foreign-controlled firms bear a

heavier fiscal burden than their Canadian-owned counterparts should not be too difficult to devise. Statutory requirements that foreign firms operating in Canada should
make shares in their Canadian subsidiaries available for
purchase by Canadians would have much the same result.
So would requirements for Canadian representation on
boards of directors, for the employment of stipulated percentages of Canadian citizens on the work force, and for
the public disclosure of all transactions between subsidiaries and parents. Restrictions, or the threat of restrictions, on the repatriation of earnings from Canadian
subsidiaries would also have a discouraging effect. And
there are good precedents in Canadian history for restrictions on the export of Canadian produce in unmanufactured state, either by export tariffs or by discriminatory
royalty arrangements. The possibility of retaliation by the
United States must, of course, be borne in mind in con-
templating any of these policies, and the administrative
difficulties might be severe; but one can hardly deny that
the possibilities exist. Serious official discussion of the
possibilities might, indeed, be sufficient in itself to produce
the desired result, since it would introduce into the
situation an element of uncertainty that has so far been
absent.

If such relatively moderate measures are insufficient,
there is always the *ultima ratio* of expropriation and nationalization. Canada has the right, fully recognized by
international law, to take over any foreign-owned property
within her jurisdiction, upon payment of appropriate com-
pensation. Recent history has shown that this right can
be exercised with impunity. Mexico's nationalization of
foreign oil properties in 1938 gave that country a prolonged respite from American investment; and more
recently Cuba has given unmistakable evidence of antip-

athy to foreign ownership and control. But sentiment in Canada will have to change considerably before such examples as these are followed. Canadians may grumble about the extent of foreign control; they may even discuss, in an academic way, what might be done to reduce it. They are not likely, however, to act in a way that clearly and obviously injures their economic interests, or their image of Canada as a guardian of international morality. It is notable, indeed, that the policies that have been advocated in Canada to reduce dependence on foreign resources involve, not aggressive action against others, but rather self-discipline and self-restraint. Canadians, for example, must learn to live within their means; they must not borrow excessively from others; they must save more and avoid extravagance. Reflected in counsels such as these are the homely Scottish virtues of prudence and thrift, a morality that enjoins self-improvement, not hostility to others, as the remedy for discontent.

It is not necessary, however, to rely on unprovable assertions about national character to demonstrate that drastic action to limit American investment or the activities of American corporations is, in Canada, improbable. The structure of Canadian government is in itself such as to make effective action in this direction very difficult. The inflow of American capital, as we have seen, is channeled into three principal sectors of the Canadian economy: the resource industries, secondary manufacturing, and governments. In each of these cases, there are provincial and regional interests involved that would certainly resist strongly and effectively any moves by the federal government to restrict their access to American capital. Equally strong regional pressures would oppose any attempt to hamper the sale of raw material exports in the American market. The federal government is and must be concerned with the preservation of Canada as a political and economic unit. This is the objective to which all its policies, directly or indirectly, must be guided. If the influence of the United States is such as to threaten this objective, the primary responsibility for defensive measures lies with the federal government, and it is at this level that the pressures will be felt. The provincial governments, on the other hand, are primarily concerned with advancing the interests of their particular regions and the people who live in them. The preservation of national economic and political unity is to them a secondary consideration.

We have already suggested that the essence of Canada's problem is the conflict between economic development and autonomy. Equally, however, it is a conflict between provincial and federal concepts of how economic development should come about — a conflict that remains latent as long as federal policy tends to advance the economic interests of the provinces but that becomes explicit whenever the federal government, in the interests of preserving national unity, takes action that injures or retards provincial development. There have already been several examples of this: Conspicuous cases in recent years have been the conflict with British Columbia over the hydroelectric development of the Columbia and Peace rivers, with Alberta and Saskatchewan over the construction of the Trans-Canada natural gas pipeline, and with the same two provinces over the proposed crude oil pipeline to Montreal. These are the modern counterparts of earlier controversies over railroad construction, freight rates, and the tariff. Any determined attempt by the federal government to limit the inflow of American capital or redirect Canadian trade away from the American market will produce a multitude of new federal-provincial conflicts of this kind. In the process, it is likely to subject the Canadian federation to internal stresses of considerable severity.

The difficulties stand out particularly clearly in connection with the transfer and use of Canadian natural resources. Here, the federal government has only limited jurisdiction. It controls directly the resources of the Yukon and North West Territories. Under the terms of the Canada-United States Treaty of 1909, it is responsible for determining the use made of boundary waters, though here, as in connection with offshore fisheries, provincial rights also are involved. And it exercises supervision over the export of electricity and natural gas through the National Energy Board. With these exceptions, its ability to influence the terms on which natural resources are transferred to private ownership is very small. The provinces control their own natural resources; the provincial governments, not the federal, determine the pace of resource development in Canada.

If, therefore, any attempt is to be made to retard the rate of resource development, or more specifically to retard the rate at which resources are transferred to the ownership of American-controlled corporations, it must be made at the provincial, not the federal, level. This in itself is enough to make the probability of any such attempt very small. The provinces, if one may speak generally, are little concerned with the broad national considerations that, from the federal point of view, might make some slowing-down in the alienation of Canadian resources seem desirable. On the contrary, if past history is any guide, their policies have tended to favor the maximum amount of resource development in the shortest possible time, and the nationality of the interests to whom resources are sold or leased has been a very minor consideration. There are exceptions, most of them reflecting provincial attempts to establish processing industries, but by and large the attitude of the provincial governments has been that natural resources should be discovered as quickly as possible, that when discovered they should be developed as quickly as possible, and that all this should be done on the largest possible scale.

However improvident or short-sighted such an attitude may seem from the federal point of view, it is hardly unreasonable. The whole development of the Canadian economy has been based upon the exploitation of a seemingly endless supply of natural resources available at little cost. The idea that the maximum rate of resource development may not necessarily be the optimum rate has been slow in emerging at the federal level and has made little impress on provincial policies. Nor is it to be expected that provincial governments would take kindly to the suggestion that the rate at which their resources are developed should be deliberately retarded. From the provincial point of view, there is little reason why it should. Resource development means greater employment opportunities, larger payrolls, a more diversified economic base, larger taxable capacity, and buoyant provincial revenues. And there are substantial political advantages to be gained also, for the party in power and for individual politicians, in terms of prestige, a reputation for "getting things done," and sometimes in more tangible forms. Fundamental is the belief that resource development is good and anything that retards or prevents resource development bad, an attitude typical of societies that regard natural resources as in effect free goods.

Nothing would do more to check the flow of direct investment capital into Canada and the growth of foreign ownership in the Canadian economy than a deliberate slowing-down of resource development. But to ask the provincial governments to adopt such a policy is to ask the impossible. A deliberate retarding of resource development, a deliberate stiffening of the terms under which resources are sold or leased to private interests, requires both the ability to wait and the willingness to do so. Few provincial governments are in a position to bear the costs of waiting, and few provincial politicians willing to bear the onus of assuming the costs. Their bargaining position is typically weak, pressure for rapid development severe, and elections never far distant. Above all, from the provincial point of view, there is no clear and present reason why they should wait. The reasons are evident only at the federal level, and even there only on one particular interpretation of the national interest. If continental economic integration is in any sense a threat, it is a threat to Canada as a nation. It is not a threat to the provinces as such, many of whom, dependent as they are on American capital and the American market, would find it easier to defend their regional economic interests if they had two senators apiece in the United States Congress than they do at present, when all pressure on the United States government must be exerted through Ottawa.

Even at the federal level, there is at present no agreement that the inflow of American capital presents any significant threat to Canada. The Governor of the Bank of Canada may anathematize the "do it all now at any cost" approach to economic development; but the Minister of Trade and Commerce sees no reason for concern. Federal politicians are dependent on provincial support, and a party that came to power on the strength of a new vision of Canada's future inevitably finds the prospect of a deliberate retarding of economic growth somewhat disconcerting to contemplate. Even if there were a consensus that resource development was proceeding at too fast a pace, or on terms unfavorable to Canada, it is hard to see what the federal government could do about it, beyond abandoning certain development projects, such as the "roads to resources" program, to which it is already committed. It is true that Canada's tax structure is at present designed to encourage foreign investment, and that in a variety of ways it could be adjusted to lean in the opposite direction. It is true also that the resource industries have been granted special treatment under the tax laws (such as the exemption of producing mines from taxation for the first three years) and that these privileges could be withdrawn or confined to Canadian-owned firms. And it is true that much of the large-scale public investment undertaken by the federal government in recent years, such as the St. Lawrence Seaway, the South Saskatchewan dam, and (indirectly) the Trans-Canada gas pipeline, have had a developmental purpose; similar programs could be delayed or abandoned in the future. But these possibilities, if they are to be realized, demand a consistency of purpose, a strength of conviction, and a willingness to accept political and economic sacrifices that do not at present seem to exist. If the pace of resource development in Canada does slow down in the near future, it is unlikely to be the result of any actions of the federal government; the more probable causes are a major depression, a diversion of American direct investment to other areas, or a significant reduction in expenditures on armaments.

Granted that the process of continental economic integration can be accelerated or retarded and that policies designed to achieve either goal are not difficult to devise, however difficult they might be to implement, one may still ask, for the United States and for Canada, in which direction the national interest lies. This is the kind of question which social scientists are always ready to raise but which, if they are prudent, they are reluctant to answer. Whether a given policy is in the national interest depends upon the benefits expected from that policy and the costs that will be incurred if the policy is adopted. To a greater or less degree, these costs and benefits are always subjective: They can be weighed and compared only by the individuals and groups directly affected. An objective analyst, if he is to live up to his mandate, must refrain from impertinent attempts to make up other people's minds for them. The most he can do is insure, as best he can, that the implications of alternative policies are not ignored and that inconsistencies in choice are avoided.

As far as the United States is concerned, the matter can be disposed of relatively briefly. The fact that economic integration with Canada has already proceeded so far is itself evidence that, over a long period, individual American businessmen, corporations, and investors have found it in their interests to trade with Canada, develop Canadian resources, and produce for the Canadian market. In no meaningful sense can this historical process be described as having been contrary to the national interest of the United States. It has enlarged the resource base for American industry, the market for American manufactures, and the American labor supply. For the past fifty years at least, Canada has been one of the American economy's richest frontiers — a frontier of untapped resources and generous profit opportunities. And, until recently, it has been a frontier that, for the United States, presented no serious problems.

Even today it can still be said that Canada presents no serious problems, at least in comparison with the problems that harass the United States in its relations with other countries. Frictions there may be; protests against one policy or another; and an undercurrent of resentment that can hardly be ignored by anyone concerned with the image that the United States presents to the rest of the world. But, just as the process of continental integration in the past began and moved ahead almost imperceptibly and without conscious direction, so today it continues as a matter of private, day-to-day decisions, accelerated to some extent by the insecurity associated with investment in other areas and by the cumulative growth of the American demand for raw materials, but still a gradual process, entirely nonpolitical in its objectives and execution. There is no obvious reason at present why the United States should attempt either to accelerate or to retard this process.

If, in the past, economic integration with Canada has been in the national interest of the United States, and if it promises to be so in the future also, it is highly desirable that the United States should avoid policies that interfere with this process. For example, it is difficult to see any reasonable justification for tariff and quota restrictions on the importation of Canadian raw materials. Such restrictions are in effect subsidies to particular sectors of the American domestic economy. They raise the cost of raw materials to American industry, maintain in existence marginal sources of supply which could not survive in open competition, and inhibit a rational allocation of capital and labor. One might find something to be said in their favor if they were in the nature of adjustment subsidies — temporary measures, that is to say, designed to reduce the difficulties of regions whose resource base has become depleted and to facilitate the transfer of labor and capital to other more productive employments. But these are not the terms in which they have been presented to the American public and the outside world.

Alternatively, one might reasonably defend such restrictive measures if dependence on imports of certain raw materials entailed serious strategic risk in the event of war. But arguments of this kind cannot apply to Canada, and only a slavish commitment to the principle of non-discrimination can explain why restrictions imposed because of strategic risk are applied to areas where no such risk exists. Canadian raw materials are today, in peace or war, an invaluable supplement to the resource base of the American economy. Policies that restrict the importation of these raw materials are undesirable, not because they irritate Canadians, but because they are contrary to the interests of the United States.

Problems of this type are likely to arise with increasing frequency in the future as requirements for raw materials continue to grow and domestic resources within the United States become more and more depleted. It is true that scientific progress has in the past successfully offset many of the unfortunate consequences of resource depletion and probably will continue to do so. And it is also true that, in comparison with other factors tending to burden American industry with a high level of costs, resource depletion may be of relatively minor importance and certainly is less conspicuous in its influence. Nevertheless, much depends on the way in which American policy responds to the problem of resource depletion. On the one hand, policy can be directed toward encouraging the development of foreign sources of supply by the exporting of American capital, technical skills, and managerial experience. On the other, policy can turn inward, toward the protection of dwindling domestic sources of supply, relying on scientific advance and technical ingenuity to counteract the inescapable tendencies toward rising costs. At present, the United States appears to be trying to follow both policies at the same time. New sources of raw materials are created by American foreign investment; and these same raw materials, once they become available, are excluded from the American market by tariffs and quotas designed to protect the domestic industry. In terms of domestic politics, the attractions of an autarkic, isolationist resources policy are very great, particularly in a period of serious international tension. The more outward-looking, expansive policies, however, promise greater long-run benefits both to the United States and to its allies.

When we turn to Canada, judgment becomes much more difficult. If we ask whether it is possible for Canada to resist continental economic integration, the answer must be in the affirmative. A variety of policies are available to limit United States investment, restrict the activities of United States-controlled firms, retard the rate of exploitation of Canadian resources by United States interests, and counteract the tendency for Canadian trade to become increasingly concentrated on American suppliers and the American market. But would it be desirable for Canada to adopt such policies? What are the probable benefits and what the probable costs? Appraisal of these issues must necessarily be very tentative.

The costs of serious attempts to inhibit continental integration would be high, so high, in fact, as to render the political feasibility of any such attempts very doubtful. The process has already gone very far and the Canadian economy has become adjusted to it. Attempts to halt or reverse the tendencies now dominant would cause serious economic disturbance: large-scale unemployment in industries producing for the American market; stagnation and decline in regions whose development is geared to the inflow of American capital; and an over-all retardation of the rate of economic development in Canada. The fundamental consideration, as we have already emphasized, is that no alternative strategy of economic development is available. An economy such as Canada's, highly specialized in international trade, cannot shut itself off from the outside world and hope to survive. It must exploit the opportunities for economic development that are presented to it. These opportunities in present circumstances imply closer integration with the United States.

So great would be the costs involved in a serious attempt to halt economic integration that it is tempting to describe the task as impossible. This, however, is an overstatement. The possibilities do exist. It is true that, if any steps were taken to realize them at present, serious political difficulties would arise, not only at the federal level but also between the federal government and the provinces. And it is undeniable that the economic disturbances likely to result would make the decline of the Canadian uranium industry when United States purchase contracts expired seem like a minor setback. But this merely serves to emphasize the fact that, if positive steps are taken to check economic integration, they will be taken only under severe provocation and in pursuit of objectives that are regarded as worthy of great sacrifices.

What then are the benefits expected to follow from a retarding of continental integration? And are these expectations well founded? At the cost of some oversimplification, the principal anticipated benefit can be described as greater freedom of action. The question is, then, whether resistance to continental integration would be likely to increase Canada's freedom of action in any significant degree.

It is essential in this connection to distinguish clearly between limitations on Canada's freedom of action that stem directly from the United States and those that arise merely because Canadians are living in the twentieth century. It may be possible to counteract the first type of restrictive influence, but the second is somewhat harder to deal with. Canada at present, like most other nations, finds itself caught up in a situation in which the range of alternative feasible courses of action is small. Economically and politically, present choices are limited by choices made earlier in time, by the choices of other sovereign states, and by the growing interdependence of human affairs in a world that daily grows smaller and more crowded. The impact of industrialism, mass literacy, scientific discovery, and the commercialization of culture is universal: No nation can hope to insulate itself from these pressures, and all nations find their freedom of action limited by the need to accommodate to them.

Granted that there exist tendencies which, if they persist, will integrate Canada's economy more and more intimately with that of the United States, and granted that these tendencies cannot be halted by Canada without serious internal difficulties, are these tendencies likely to reduce Canada's political freedom of action, internally and externally, to any significant extent? Those who answer this question with a confident affirmative overlook the correspondence, in the years since the end of World War II, between Canada's increasing stature in international affairs and its increasing economic integration with the United States. If recent history is any guide, the two developments are by no means inconsistent with one another. Canada now plays a much more positive role in international affairs and enjoys more respect as an international power than at any previous point in its history; yet, economically, it is more dependent on the United States than it ever was before. Is this a paradox?

Only superficially: Canada's role in international politics depends more on the caliber of its diplomats, on the skill with which it participates in negotiations, and on the practical utility of its proposals than on the economic opportunities on which its development is based.

As for Canada's internal politics, the most serious and at the same time most prevalent fallacy is to identify economic integration with annexation or political absorption. This idea, as we have already argued, will not withstand serious analysis. Economic integration does not necessarily imply political integration and can proceed very far without any sacrifice of formal sovereignty by either party. In many fields of domestic government policy (property and civil rights, education, religion, and language), the degree of economic integration with the United States is a neutral factor. In others (trade and investment, transportation, immigration, resource development, and monetary and fiscal policy), relations with the United States are undoubtedly of vital importance, but no cession of Canadian sovereignty is involved. In economic policy particularly, Canada's freedom of action is certainly limited, but the limiting factor is, in the last analysis, Canada's own acceptance of full employment and rapid economic development as high-priority social objectives. As long as these objectives command the adherence that is at present accorded them, Canada has little choice but to exploit the opportunities for development that present themselves. Other policies are conceivable but not politically acceptable. The political unacceptability of alternative policies reflects, in this instance, not a doctrinaire commitment to particular political programs but a general social preference for prosperity and economic expansion rather than the more intangible dividends of nationalism. As long as this preference persists, it will continue to be politically expedient to talk about resisting economic integration, but politically suicidal to do anything about it.

To Canada's formal sovereignty there is no threat. Any encroachment in this respect, direct or indirect, is certain to be resisted vigorously. The violent Canadian reaction when the Ford Motor Company of Canada was prevented from exporting automobiles to Communist China, because if it did its parent company might have been liable to prosecution under United States law, illustrates the point, as do the recurrent complaints when Canadian politicians find it difficult to gain access to American bases on Canadian soil. This is a very sensitive area of Canadian sentiment, and there seems little danger that Canada will find the formal aspects of its sovereignty imperceptibly whittled away. The prospect is rather that scope for the effective exercise of sovereignty may become more and more circumscribed as integration, economic and strategic, proceeds. It is useless to argue that such a development is not highly probable. The parameters of choice are becoming increasingly restrictive and in one area after another it begins to seem as if there is only one direction in which Canada can move. This is not a prospect that Canadians find congenial. Yet, though the dilemma may be more stark for Canada than for other countries, the progressive erosion of the effective powers of the nation state is a phenomenon not restricted to Canada and not to be ascribed solely to Canada's economic dependence on the United States. There is no nation in the western alliance which can hope to find security by relying on its own resources and defending its own frontiers. For defense as for development regional groupings in some form have come to be indispensable.

If this analysis of current trends has any validity, it would appear that Canada can hardly hope to avoid integration into some broader complex of nation states in some form or other, with the limitations on the effective exercise of national sovereignty that such integration implies. The issue narrows down, therefore, to what form of integration it is expedient to adopt, and which other nation states are to be included. Though seldom expressed in precisely these terms, this problem has in fact arisen with some regularity in the postwar years and a consistent pattern has emerged. Canadian policy has had as one of its foundation stones support of the United Nations, and it may be surmised that there would be less resistance to the conversion of the United Nations into a truly supranational body, with its own armed forces, in Canada than in most other countries. This, however, does not appear in present circumstances to be an attainable goal. Consistently, too, Canada has attempted to maintain and support the Commonwealth, using it as a means of allocating aid to underdeveloped countries, negotiating on trade issues, and coordinating foreign policy. Canada has also been one of the strongest supporters of the General Agreement on Tariffs and Trade and has lived up to its commitments under the Agreement as conscientiously as most other nations. Similarly, Canadian statesmen have consistently supported the idea of converting the North Atlantic Treaty Organization into something more than a military alliance, in particular by extending its functions into the economic sphere. Such a reinterpretation of the purposes and functions of NATO may have been feasible at one time, but is so no longer. Supporters of NATO are finding it a difficult enough task to maintain the original conception of a pooling of armed forces without undertaking additional responsibilities. More recently, with the appearance of the European Common Market and the Free Trade Area, there have been proposals, mostly from spokesmen of the Liberal Party, that Canada should support the formation of a North Atlantic free trade area. What this would involve has not as yet been specified, but presumably it would include the United States and Canada as well as both European trading blocs.

The feasibility of such a proposal is questionable, particularly if it is contingent upon the participation of the United States. For present purposes, however, it is sufficient to emphasize that Canada has, in the postwar period, consistently attempted to offset its growing economic involvement with the United States by strengthening its economic, military, and diplomatic connections with other countries, and particularly with Europe. On the other hand, Canada has shown little inclination to make common cause with other Western Hemisphere countries, and in particular has so far declined to join the Organization of American States. If this pattern of behavior continues, we may expect Canada to place no serious obstacle in the way of closer economic integration with the United States, and to rely primarily on the United States for the strategic security of the continent, but at the same time to pursue consistently a policy of strengthening economic, political, and military ties with Europe. The proposed North Atlantic free trade area is merely an idealization of the general objective; if it does not prove feasible, other techniques for involving Canada in European affairs and Europe in Canadian affairs will be found. The strategy is one of exploiting to the full the economic benefits of proximity to the United States while neutralizing as far as possible the political and cultural consequences of economic integration by the maintenance of the European connection. Canada, in short, is attempt-

ing to bring in the Old World to redress the balance of
the New. Whether the strategy will prove effective or
not in the long run depends primarily on the future
growth of the European economies, the policies they
adopt with reference to North American trade and investment, and, needless to add, the avoidance of a major
war.

A strategy such as this may enable Canada to retain
some freedom of action in the political and economic
spheres. Whether it will serve to protect and foster a
distinctively Canadian way of life is more doubtful. But
here again a distinction must be made between pressures
upon Canada that emanate specifically from the United
States and those that have a more general origin. The
major threat to the survival of distinctive cultural values
in Canada is not the United States as such but twentieth-
century industrialism, particularly the industrialization
of communications. If Canada were less intimately involved in an economic sense with the United States, the
pressures for uniformity in thought and action would
still persist, though perhaps in more moderate form.
Nations with cultural traditions far richer and more
respected than Canada's are at present experiencing
difficulties of much the same kind. They at least are in
a position to fight a rear-guard action, defending a sense
of cultural identity and difference that already exists. It
is Canada's misfortune that she must attempt to develop
a cultural tradition of her own at a time in the world's
history when all the tendencies of technology and commercialization are working against her.

The forces which are tending to shape all societies of
the western world into a common mold are not specifically American in origin. The United States is, however,
undoubtedly the leading contemporary example of the

model to which all are increasingly tending to conform. It is natural, therefore, to argue that it is the cultural influence of the United States that is to be resisted. In Canada, in particular, this argument has an insidious plausibility. Americans and Canadians share many of the same values; their lives follow very similar patterns; the differences between the two national cultures, to the extent that they exist, are matters of degree, of relatively minor variations on a common theme. It is easy for Canadians to assert that this correspondence is the result of American cultural imperialism, of the massive and unremitting exposure of Canadians to American standards and the American communications industries. Yet, is it not equally plausible to believe that what we see here is a common North American cultural pattern, a pattern on which both Americans and Canadians have embroidered a few distinctive variations but which nevertheless is the heritage and the creation of both? Is it true that the emergence of a distinctively Canadian culture has been suppressed by the influence of the United States? Or should we not rather say that the United States and Canada, springing from the same cultural roots and experiencing the same process of continental expansion, have evolved a way of life that is congenial to both?

However this may be, cultural interaction between the United States and Canada is already so continuous and wide-ranging that it is very doubtful whether closer economic integration could do much to accentuate its effects or resistance to economic integration reduce them. If Canadians wish to evolve a way of life that they can call their own, it must surely be not by turning their backs on the United States but rather by exploiting to the full the creative potential of North American culture and, from their own talents and resources, making a distinctive contribution to it. This is not an unrealistic objective. Economic integration does not necessarily mean cultural absorption. The existence in the United States of a single extremely complex and highly integrated national economy has not proved incompatible with the survival of distinctive regional cultures and attitudes. A Texan is still a Texan; the southern states still preserve many of their own customs and attitudes; a Californian does not think of himself as the same sort of person as a New Yorker, nor does he live in the same way. The survival and vitality of such regional differences as these — and analogous examples could be found even in the more monolithic structure of the Soviet Union — must give grounds for optimism to all who see a value in cultural variety rather than cultural uniformity.

⌐If Canadians lack faith in their ability to maintain a sense of identity in the face of economic integration with the United States, it can only be because they set a low estimate on the vitality and creativity of their own cultural life.⌐It is not enough to point to differences between the two countries in population or other measures of size. Creativity — the ability to introduce cultural variations that survive and gain acceptance — is a matter of quality, not quantity. History, as Jacob Viner has recently emphasized, gives little warrant for believing that the political and economic integration of a smaller nation into a larger one necessarily deprives the smaller of opportunity for cultural autonomy.[9] Relative size, suggests Viner, is far from a complete explanation of the extent and even the net direction of cultural influence on each other of neighboring peoples with a common language. Scotland was "teacher of the world" during most of the eighteenth century. German Austria, particularly Vienna, exercised a remarkable cultural influence on Germany and on Europe as a whole from the 1870's to the 1920's. And the tiny Swiss canton of Geneva from the time of Calvin produced a steady stream of thinkers of international reputation whose contribution to European science and literature was out of all proportion to the economic resources of the canton itself. Mere size cannot explain cultural vitality of this kind. Political and economic integration with a larger unit does not rule out cultural autonomy; it may indeed provide an environment that is highly favorable.

Could Canada in the twentieth century come to exercise cultural leadership in North America as Scotland, Austria, and Geneva once did in Europe? We know too little about the factors that determine why and where learning and the creative arts flourish to permit a confident answer. But the possibility is not to be dismissed offhand, and certainly not for any reasons connected with economic integration. Far more relevant are such considerations as the quality of Canada's educational system, the support and toleration granted to artists and creative thinkers, and the extent to which talent and originality are recognized and encouraged wherever they may be found. There is no reason to suppose that economic integration with the United States, whether on a continental basis or in some more inclusive system, would affect such factors as these. The danger is rather that resistance to economic integration may engender in Canada a narrow introspective nationalism which, by its insistence on defense against external threats, may stultify the very sources of internal creativity that should be encouraged. Canada's best defense of its identity lies not in a rejection of challenges from the outside but in an emphasis on the quality of its response.

It may be that the future holds for Canada no better prospect than gradual absorption by the United States, a slow but cumulative process of integration that, beginning with the mundane affairs of trade and investment and the unfortunate imperatives of continental defense, finally leaves to Canada no more than the empty form of sovereignty. If this is indeed the outcome, more than Canadians will be the losers, for anything that reduces the variety and interest of human experience does damage to all. Many Canadians today believe that this is in fact the prospect that faces them; small wonder, then, that each step on the road is regarded at best with resignation, at worst with resentment.

Yet it is possible that the outcome may be very different. Economic integration has brought tremendous benefits to Canada, and continues to do so. It is unlikely that the process will encounter serious resistance. What will be resisted will be any tendencies for the process to broaden beyond the economic sphere. These tendencies are, of course, ubiquitous and constant. For this reason, conflict also is ubiquitous and constant. It is not in Canada's interests that these conflicts should cease or be concealed, for it is through them that Canadians assert their independence, reinforce their sense of solidarity, and above all exercise a constant pressure to confine economic relationships to a narrow field in which the interests of the two countries do in fact coincide. Only by unremitting scrutiny and criticism can Canadians take advantage of economic integration while at the same time maintaining their political independence and preserving their sense of cultural difference. What type of relationship between the two countries will finally emerge it is impossible to predict. But one may hazard the guess that it will be a relationship that makes it possible for Canadians still to call themselves Canadians, and still to think of themselves as in some way — a way perhaps better left undefined — different from their neighbors to the south.

Appendix

United States Direct Investment Companies in Canada: Sources and Allocation of Funds

Balance-of-payments statistics of the inflow of United States direct investment capital into Canada give an incomplete picture of the role played by American-controlled firms in Canadian capital formation and therefore in Canadian economic development. The capital inflow series relate primarily to the international transactions in which Canada is engaged. If we wish to estimate the scope and impact of the investment activities of American-controlled firms, we must supplement the capital inflow statistics by other information. Ideally, we should like to measure the total funds available to such firms. Funds that cross the border and are reported in balance-of-payments statistics are only one component of this total. American-controlled firms utilize for investment and other business purposes large volumes of funds generated internally in their day-to-day business as well as funds secured from capital markets and other external sources in Canada.

Figures published by the Dominion Bureau of Statistics throw little light on this question. Estimates are available of the retained profits of foreign direct investments in Canada,

but not on a country-by-country basis.[1] Other sources of
funds, such as depreciation and depletion allowances, are not
separately reported. Account is taken of the fact that the
annual net increase in the book value of United States direct
investments in Canada differs significantly from the annual
gross inflow of new capital, but the items responsible for the
difference are not presented in such a way as to make clear
where the funds come from.

The United States Department of Commerce has thrown
new light on this obscure area as a result of an annual survey,
initiated in 1957, of the sources of funds of foreign subsidiaries of United States companies.[2] The foreign enterprises
covered represent, in terms of earnings, about four-fifths of
all United States direct foreign investments. For Canada, the
coverage is 78 per cent of the total. The data obtained are
intended to supplement the available information on net
private capital movements from the United States and to
make possible more satisfactory measures of the investment
activity of United States-controlled foreign enterprises than
can be derived from balance-of-payments statistics.

The information provided by the survey has emphasized
strongly the important role played by internally generated

TABLE 33

United States Direct Foreign Investments,
Sources of Funds, 1957 and 1958

(US$ billions)

Source	1957	1958
Funds from United States	1.33	0.76
Funds obtained abroad	1.06	0.73
Depreciation and depletion	1.17	1.34
Net income	2.63	2.19
Other	0.10	0.12
Total funds available	6.29	5.15

Source. U.S. Dept. of Commerce, *Survey of Current Business*, vol·
39, no. 10 (October 1959), pp. 18–19, Table 1.
Note: Details may not add to totals because of rounding.

funds (particularly retained earnings and depreciation allowances) in financing the growth of United States firms in foreign countries. Table 33 presents the totals for 1957 and 1958.

Net United States financing accounted for only 20 per cent of the total funds available in 1957 and 15 per cent in 1958. Internal sources (net income plus depreciation and depletion) were responsible for 60 per cent and 68 per cent of total funds in the same two years.[3]

Analogous statistics are available for United States direct investments in Canada alone. They disclose that the firms covered in the sample had at their disposal US$1,506 million in 1957 and US$1,248 million in 1958. The statistics for the year 1958 are presented in Table 34. Most of these funds were generated internally. Receipts from the United States accounted for only 26 per cent of the total funds available in all sectors.

TABLE 34

United States Direct Investments in Canada, Sources of Funds, 1958
(US$ millions)

Source	Total	Mining and smelting	Petro- leum	Manu- facturing	Trade	Agricul- ture and utilities
Funds from United States	326	57	247	42	−16	−4
Funds obtained in Canada	84	−7	57	9	4	22
Depreciation and depletion	397	20	170	183	18	5
Net income	387	62	61	224	33	7
Other	54	—[a]	43	5	3	2
Total funds available	1,248	132	578	463	42	32

Source. U.S. Dept. of Commerce, *Survey of Current Business*, vol. 39, no. 10 (October 1959), p. 18, Table 1.
[a] Less than US$500,000.
Note: Minus signs denote outflows of funds on balance.

These statistics serve to emphasize the fact that the net annual inflow of direct investment capital from the United States is a totally inadequate measure of the ability of American-controlled direct investment firms to influence the allocation of resources in Canada. The Dominion Bureau of Statistics estimates of the extent of direct foreign financing of Canadian investment (see above pp. 61–62) take account of this fact by adding to the direct investment inflow estimates of retained earnings on foreign direct investments, new issues of Canadian securities sold to nonresidents, other long-term financing, changes in accounts payable, and depreciation and depletion allowances.[4] The Department of Commerce survey uses a different approach that focuses on the total funds that American-controlled corporations have at their disposal, including funds raised in Canada. The D.B.S. approach has the virtue of emphasizing the relative importance, in the aggregate, of non-Canadian resources, but the Department of Commerce method probably demonstrates more effectively the leverage that American-controlled firms exercise.

The survey also yields information on the use made of these funds. For all United States direct foreign investments, the allocation of funds in 1957 and 1958 was as shown in

TABLE 35

United States Direct Foreign Investments, Uses of Funds, 1957 and 1958
(US$ billions)

Use	1957	1958
Property, plant, and equipment	3.47	2.99
Inventories	0.59	−0.11
Receivables	0.40	0.19
Other assets	0.21	0.35
Income paid out	1.62	1.73
Total funds allocated	6.29	5.15

Source. U.S. Dept. of Commerce, *Survey of Current Business*, vol. 39, no. 10 (October 1959), p. 19, Table 1.
Note: Minus signs denote net disinvestment.

Table 35. About 88 per cent of the funds available after income disbursements in 1958 was expended on property, plant, and equipment. The corresponding ratio for 1957 was approximately 75 per cent. Income payments represented about one-quarter of total funds available in the earlier year and a little over one-third in the later one.

For American direct investment firms in Canada, the corresponding figures for 1958 are presented in Table 36.

TABLE 36

United States Direct Investments in Canada, Uses of Funds, 1958
(US$ millions)

Use	Total	Mining and smelting	Petro-leum	Manu-facturing	Trade	Agri-culture and utilities
Property, plant, and equipment	914	119	480	272	19	25
Inventories	−87	−5	−20	−64	2	−1
Receivables	44	−13	30	24	2	1
Other assets	105	−15	23	88	4	5
Income paid out	272	46	65	143	15	2
Total funds allocated	1,248	132	578	463	42	32

Source. U.S. Dept. of Commerce, *Survey of Current Business*, vol. 39, no. 10 (October 1959), p. 19, Table 1.
Note: Minus signs denote net disinvestment.

The proportion of the total (after income payments) allocated to property, plant, and equipment was no less than 94 per cent for all sectors.[5] Income payments represented 22 per cent of all funds allocated.

Clearly the gross investments of American-controlled firms in Canada are much larger than the statistics of capital inflows and retained profits would suggest. Total receipts of funds from the United States in 1958, for the direct investment firms in Canada covered in the survey, amounted to only

US$326 million; the net increase in book value (receipts of
funds from the United States plus retained earnings) was
US$441 million; yet in the same year expenditures on property,
plant, and equipment amounted to US$914 million. Nor is
there any clear relationship between fluctuations in investment expenditures and fluctuations in the sum of capital inflows and retained earnings. Receipts of funds from the
United States plus retained earnings fell by 36 per cent
between 1957 and 1958; expenditures on property, plant, and
equipment declined in the same period by only 18 per cent.[6]

Balance-of-payments statistics are designed to record international transactions. They are not intended to reflect the
internal allocations of funds within integrated enterprises. Yet
the relative weight of American-controlled firms in the Canadian economy can be gauged only by taking into account the
total volume of expenditures for which they are responsible
and the total volume of funds whose allocation they can
determine. For this purpose balance-of-payments statistics of
international capital flows, even when supplemented by estimates of the retained earnings of direct investment companies,
are an inadequate guide. It is to be hoped that, as the Department of Commerce sample survey is continued for successive
years and its conclusions extended by the broader survey
of American business investments in foreign countries currently in progress, we shall be provided with a firmer statistical basis for judgment than is at present available.

Notes

CHAPTER I. *Regional Integration and Economic Development*

1. If a commercial agreement between two countries, A and B, includes an unconditional most-favored-nation clause, any concession granted by A to a third country, C, is automatically granted to B also. The tendency is therefore to generalize tariff reductions among all nations bound together by most-favored-nation agreements. On the other hand, such agreements make bilateral tariff negotiations between any single pair of countries (such as the United States and Canada) very difficult.

2. The literature on the theory of economic integration is already large. See particularly Jacob Viner, *The Customs Union Issue* (New York, 1950); Tibor Scitovsky, *Economic Theory and Western European Integration* (London, 1958); Harry G. Johnson, "The Economic Gains from Freer Trade with Europe," *Three Banks Review*, no. 39 (September 1958); and Richard E. Caves, "Europe's Unification and Canada's Trade," *Canadian Journal of Economics and Political Science*, vol. 25, no. 3 (August 1959), pp. 249–258.

3. The economic integration of two or more areas may be defined as a process which brings into existence a single market for commodities and for factors of production. In Europe, the creation of a common market for commodities has attracted most attention. In North America, however, the absence of significant barriers to the movement of capital, labor, and entrepreneurship has been the more important factor in integration. A case could be made for the view that a single market for the factors of production is the more critical element in integration, since it permits a better spatial allocation of scarce

resources. Mobility of goods, as Ohlin has pointed out, compensates for the lack of mobility of factors, but only to a limited extent. See Bertil Ohlin, *Interregional and International Trade* (Cambridge, Mass., 1933), p. 42.

4. Grant L. Reuber, *The Growth and Changing Composition of Trade between Canada and the United States* (Montreal: Canadian-American Committee, 1960), pp. 8–17.

5. U.S. Dept. of Commerce, *Statistical Abstract of the United States: 1959* (Washington, D.C., 1959), pp. 894–895, Table no. 1178.

6. U.S. Dept. of Commerce, *Survey of Current Business* (August 1959), p. 29, Table 1.

7. Dominion Bureau of Statistics, *Canadian Balance of International Payments, 1958, and International Investment Position* (Ottawa, 1959), p. 61, Table XIII. All dollar figures in this book refer to Canadian currency unless there is a statement to the contrary.

8. *Ibid.*, pp. 46–47, Table II, and p. 40, statement 20.

9. President's Materials Policy Commission, *Resources for Freedom* (the *Paley Report*), 5 vols. (Washington, D.C., 1952).

10. John J. Deutsch, "Recent American Influence in Canada," in Duke University Commonwealth-Studies Center, *The American Economic Impact on Canada* (Durham, N.C., 1959), pp. 36–50.

CHAPTER II. *American Capital in Canada: The Statistical Evidence*

1. *Cf.* C. P. Kindleberger, *International Short Term Capital Movements* (New York, 1937), p. 3; J. A. Stovel, *Canada in the World Economy* (Cambridge, Mass., 1959), p. 25.

2. Dominion Bureau of Statistics, *The Canadian Balance of International Payments: A Study of Methods and Results* (Ottawa, 1939), pp. 28–33; Irving Brecher and S. S. Riesman, *Canada-United States Economic Relations* (Ottawa, 1957), pp. 90–91.

3. D.B.S., *Canada's International Investment Position, 1926–1954* (Ottawa, 1958), p. 24; Brecher and Riesman, *op. cit.*, p. 90.

4. D.B.S., *The Canadian Balance of International Payments, 1926 to 1948* (Ottawa, 1949), pp. 15–16.

5. D.B.S., *Canadian Balance: Methods and Results*, pp. 19–20.

6. H. C. Pentland, "The Role of Capital in Canadian Economic Development before 1875," *Canadian Journal of Economics and Political Science*, vol. 16, no. 4 (November 1950), pp. 457–474; and "Further Observations on Canadian Development," *ibid.*, vol. 19, no. 3 (August 1953), pp. 403–410.

7. Leland H. Jenks, *The Migration of British Capital to 1875* (New York and London, 1927), pp. 66, 73–74, 85. See also Penelope Hartland, "Private Enterprise and International Capital," *Canadian Journal*

American Capital in Canada 205

of Economics and Political Science, vol. 19, no. 1 (February 1953), pp. 70–80; and, for a discussion of the relative abilities of Canada and the United States to attract British capital, H. G. J. Aitken, "A Note on the Capital Resources of Upper Canada," *Canadian Journal of Economics and Political Science*, vol. 18, no. 4 (November 1952), pp. 525–533.

8. Penelope Hartland, "Canadian Balance of Payments since 1868," in National Bureau of Economic Research, *Trends in the American Economy in the Nineteenth Century*, Studies in Income and Wealth, vol. 24 (Princeton: Princeton University Press for the National Bureau of Economic Research, 1960), pp. 717–753. The indirect estimate of the net capital inflow is obtained by summing the annual estimates of the net balance on current account, not the five-year moving averages shown in Table 2.

9. O. J. Firestone, *Canada's Economic Development 1867–1953* (London, 1958), p. 68, Table 11.

10. Compare, for example, U.S. Dept. of Commerce, *Trade Information Bulletin No. 731*, "America's Direct Investments in Foreign Countries" (Washington, 1929), p. 37, which estimates total U.S. foreign investments in 1900 at only US$500 million; and Nathaniel Bacon, "American International Indebtedness," *Yale Review* (November 1900), pp. 268–285, which sets the total (including life insurance guarantee investments) at US$501 million in the same year.

11. Jacob Viner, *Canada's Balance*.

12. Hartland, "Canadian Balance." Hartland's modifications to Viner's figures arise from (1) setting the value of Canadian investment abroad at the end of 1899 at $123.6 million (rather than $100 million), and the value of foreign investment in Canada at the end of 1899 at $1,066.0 million (rather than $1,200 million); (2) a revision in the tourist account; and (3) the elimination of certain arithmetical errors.

13. Hartland, "Canadian Balance," p. 723.

14. Total investments as shown in Table 6 do not coincide with the totals shown in Table 5 because they take no account of exports of capital from Canada and because of Hartland's corrections in the aggregates. Hartland does not provide a geographical distribution of the capital inflow for this period.

15. F. W. Field, *Capital Investments in Canada* (Toronto, 1911 and 1914).

16. From "Excursus" by Frank A. Knox in Herbert Marshall, Frank A. Southard, and Kenneth W. Taylor, *Canadian-American Industry: A Study in International Investment* (New Haven and Toronto, 1936), p. 299, Table A. Knox's own calculations, which begin in 1913, yield a total of $3,529.3 million for the accumulated annual amounts to the end of 1913, of which $2,569.3 million was from Britain, $780.0 million from the United States, and $180.0 million from all other countries.

17. Simon Kuznets, "International Differences in Capital Formation," in Moses Abramowitz (ed.), *Capital Formation and Economic Growth*, National Bureau of Economic Research Special Conference Series No. 6 (Princeton, 1955), p. 74, Table II-5.

18. Hartland, "Canadian Balance," p. 753.

19. J. A. Stovel, *Canada*, pp. 330–331.

20. Frank A. Knox, "Excursus," p. 299, Table A.

21. *Ibid.*, p. 305, Table C. Percentages refer to 1926.

22. D.B.S., *The Canadian Balance of International Payments, 1957, and International Investment Position*, p. 29, statement 17.

23. Kenneth W. Taylor, "Statistics of Foreign Trade," p. 3, in Kenneth W. Taylor and H. Michell, *Statistical Contributions to Canadian Economic History* (Toronto, 1931), vol. II; see also A. E. Safarian, *The Canadian Economy in the Great Depression* (Toronto, 1959).

24. The item listed as "net exports of non-monetary gold" in the D.B.S. current account statistics for this period is in reality Canadian gold production less Canadian consumption by industry and the arts. See D.B.S., *Canadian Balance, 1926 to 1948*, pp. 111-112. It includes, therefore, the movement of domestic gold output into official monetary reserves, which is matched in the complete balance of payments by a corresponding entry (of opposite sign) in the capital account. Penelope Hartland has argued that this procedure, though appropriate as a general method for treating gold movements, introduces significant distortion when the balance on current account is identified with the net movement of capital. She proposes, therefore, to eliminate from the current account the movement of gold into monetary reserves by adding to the net current account balance the item in the capital account which measures changes in official holdings of gold and United States dollars. See Hartland, "The Treatment of Gold in the Canadian Balance of International Payments," *Canadian Journal of Economics and Political Science*, vol. 21, no. 1 (February 1955), pp. 76–80. If this procedure were followed for the period 1926 through 1939, the net export of capital would amount to $88 million, or more than ten times the figure resulting from the official procedure.

25. D.B.S., *Canadian Balance, 1926 to 1948*, p. 181. Table XXXIII.

26. D.B.S., *Canadian Balance of International Payments, 1958* (Ottawa, 1959), p. 61, Table XIII.

27. D.B.S., *Canadian Balance, 1958*, p. 61, Table XIV. The comparison is distorted to some extent by the inclusion of petroleum and natural gas as a separate category in 1957 but not in 1939.

28. But see footnote 24 in this chapter. In the D.B.S. current account statistics, "net exports of non-monetary gold" and "gold production available for export" include the movement of gold into official reserves.

29. D.B.S., *Canadian Balance, 1958*, p. 61, Table XIII. The figure for 1958 is a preliminary estimate.

30. Quantities below the horizontal axis on this chart denote deficits in the balance on current account, or imports of capital; quantities above the horizontal axis denote surpluses, or exports of capital.

31. See C. D. Blyth, "Statistics of Canada's Balance of Payments," *Canadian Journal of Economics and Political Science*, vol. 19, no. 4 (November 1953), pp. 472–477.

32. D.B.S., *Canada's International Investment Position 1926–54*, pp.

45–47. See also A. E. Safarian and E. B. Carty, "Foreign Financing of Canadian Investment in the Post-War Period," *Proceedings of the Business and Economic Statistics Section, American Statistical Association* (September 1954), pp. 72–79.

33. D.B.S., *Canada's International Investment Position, 1926–54*, p. 46; Brecher and Riesman, *Canada-United States Economic Relations*, pp. 96–97.

34. Such a conclusion would be inescapable if there were some way of including in our calculation estimates of the capital imported by Canada in the form of adult, trained immigrants.

CHAPTER III. *The United States and the New Staples*

1. Irving Brecher and S. S. Riesman, *Canada-United States Economic Relations*, Appendix B, pp. 278–290. The percentages quoted take account of changes in control which occurred after 1953.

2. Gideon Rosenbluth has pointed out that, in terms of the proportion of national income generated, the manufacturing sector in Canada is relatively as large as that of the United States. See his *Concentration in Canadian Manufacturing Industries* (Princeton, 1957), p. 3. Canada today ranks sixth among nations in terms of income derived from manufacturing.

3. Dominion Bureau of Statistics, *Review of Foreign Trade, Calendar Year, 1958* (Ottawa, 1959), p. 18.

4. *Ibid.*, p. 62, Table IX.

5. It should not be necessary to point out that such measures in fact accelerate the depletion of domestic resources. What these protective policies are designed to conserve is not a resource but an industry. One of the political virtues of the national security argument is that it can be used to justify either conservation or resource depletion.

6. Percy W. Bidwell, *Raw Materials: A Study of American Policy* (New York, 1958), p. 1.

7. Bidwell, *Raw Materials*, p. 12.

8. *Paley Report*, vol. I, p. 5.

9. *Cf.* Edward S. Mason, "An American View of Raw-Material Problems," in *Economic Concentration and the Monopoly Problem* (Cambridge, Mass., 1957), pp. 253–275.

10. Mason, "Raw-Material Problems," pp. 264–265.

11. But see also U.S. Bureau of the Census, *Raw Materials in the United States Economy, 1900–1952* (Washington, D.C., 1954), and H. G. Aubrey, *United States Imports and World Trade* (New York, 1957).

12. Twenty-nine, that is, plus "chemicals," a general category with very great flexibility in the raw materials it utilizes.

13. *Paley Report*, vol. II, "The Outlook for Key Commodities."

Canadian aluminum was expected to supply the United Kingdom and any possible deficits in Western Europe; exports to the United States were held to depend largely on whether the benefits of lower production costs were passed on to American consumers. In the case of fluorspar, future United States requirements were expected to be met largely by synthesis from phosphate rock, rather than by imports.

14. *Paley Report*, vol. IV, "The Promise of Technology," pp. 20–21.

15. "Foreign Trade Decline Reflected in First-Quarter Balance of Payments," *Survey of Current Business* (June 1958), pp. 9–14.

16. R. A. Degen, "United States Recessions and Selected Imports," *Canadian Journal of Economics and Political Science*, vol. 25, no. 2 (May 1959), pp. 180–189.

17. Mason, "American Security and Access to Raw Materials," in *Economic Concentration and the Monopoly Problem*, pp. 224–236, at p. 226.

18. Charles E. Silberman and Lawrence A. Mayer, "The Migration of U.S. Capital," *Fortune* (January 1958), pp. 125 *ff*.

19. See U.S. Dept. of Commerce, *Factors Limiting U.S. Investment Abroad*, 2 vols. (Washington, D.C., 1954); *Paley Report*, vol. I, pp. 59–101, and vol. V, pp. 107–136.

20. This is not inconsistent with the facts that the old staples frequently required large amounts of capital, that special skills were needed, and that technological innovations were of considerable importance.

21. John H. Dales, *Hydroelectricity and Industrial Development* (Cambridge, Mass., 1957), pp. 182–183.

22. Richard E. Caves and Richard H. Holton, *The Canadian Economy: Prospect and Retrospect* (Cambridge, Mass., 1959), pp. 94–98.

23. Kenneth Buckley, *Capital Formation in Canada, 1896–1930* (Toronto, 1955), p. 128, Table A. Total new and repair construction expenditures were $78 million in 1896, $75 million in 1898, and $119 million in 1900. By 1905, they had reached $253 million.

24. Caves and Holton, *Canadian Economy*, pp. 100–101; Vernon W. Malach, *International Cycles and Canada's Balance of Payments, 1921–33* (Toronto, 1954), pp. 20–22. See also Malach, "Internal Determinants of the Canadian Upswing," *Canadian Journal of Economics and Political Science*, vol. 16, no. 2 (May 1950), pp. 184–198, and "External Determinants of the Canadian Upswing, 1921–29," *ibid.*, vol. 17, no. 1 (February 1951), pp. 50–64.

25. G. M. Meier, "Economic Development and the Transfer Mechanism: Canada, 1895–1913," *Canadian Journal of Economics and Political Science*, vol. 19, no. 1 (February 1953), pp. 1–19.

26. Caves and Holton, *Canadian Economy*, p. 103, Table 4, from D.B.S., *National Accounts, Income and Expenditure, 1926–1950* and *1950–1956*, Table 25.

27. *Ibid.*

28. Caves and Holton, *Canadian Economy*, p. 96. Note, however, the important role played by mortgage companies as channels for the flow

of foreign capital into western agriculture; for a discussion, see W. T. Easterbrook, *Farm Credit in Canada* (Toronto, 1937), and W. T. Easterbrook and Hugh G. J. Aitken, *Canadian Economic History* (Toronto, 1956), pp. 507–511.

29. The expansion of the 1920's appears to represent a "halfway house" between the pattern evident in the 1900–13 period and that evident today. In the first half of that expansion (1921–25), autonomous investment took the form of innovations in such industries as nonferrous metals, electric power, newsprint, and automobile production; these industries also absorbed large quantities of foreign capital. The second and more vigorous phase of the boom, however, did not begin until 1926, when rising prices for wheat and allied products once again stimulated expansion in the prairie region. See Malach, "External Determinants of the Canadian Upswing," p. 62.

30. See Appendix.

31. In few of the years since 1945 has the proportion of Canada's annual output devoted to capital formation fallen below 20 per cent. For comparative figures, see Simon Kuznets, "International Differences in Capital Formation," in Abramowitz, *Capital Formation*, pp. 19–106. During the period 1947–52, domestic gross capital formation was 17.9 per cent of gross national product in the United States, 13.3 per cent in the United Kingdom, and 22.5 per cent in Canada. Among industrialized countries, only Western Germany, the Netherlands, and Australia have in the postwar years had higher investment ratios than Canada.

CHAPTER IV. *The Canadian Reaction*

1. Bruce Hutchison, "Why Americans Can't Hear Canada's Hopes and Fears," *The Financial Post*, September 26, 1959.

2. Ronald B. MacPherson, *Tariffs, Markets and Economic Progress* (Toronto, 1958), p. 6.

3. Also relevant is the fragmentation of the Canadian market by subsidiaries of United States corporations, a process that results in a greater number of firms in some industries, and a smaller scale of output per firm, than would result in the absence of this type of direct investment.

4. Herbert Marshall *et al.*, *Canadian-American Industry*, pp. 233–234.

5. See R. E. Baldwin, "Patterns of Development in Newly Settled Regions," *Manchester School* (May 1954), pp. 161–179.

6. Edward S. Mason, *Economic Concentration and the Monopoly Problem*, pp. 246–247.

7. Irving Brecher and S. S. Riesman, *Canada-United States Economic Relations*, p. 121. For a discussion of these issues, see Brecher and Riesman, *op. cit.*, pp. 112–129, and William C. Hood, *Financing of Economic Activity in Canada* (Ottawa, 1958), pp. 431–458.

8. During the period 1952–58, manufacturing absorbed, on the

average, more than 17½ per cent of the gross inflow of United States direct investment capital each year. See Dominion Bureau of Statistics *Canadian Balance, 1958,* p. 25, statement 12.

9. Richard E. Caves and Richard H. Holton, *Canadian Economy,* p. xiii.

10. *First Report of the Special Study Mission to Canada of the Committee on Foreign Affairs Pursuant to House Resolution 29 (First Hays-Coffin Report),* 85th Congress, 2d Session (Washington, D.C., 1958). Actually the reclassification was to "parts of toys," not "ammunition," but the facts never caught up with the story.

11. The most concise summary of particular trouble spots in Canadian-American relations is to be found in the *First* and *Second Hays-Coffin Reports.* But see also the articles in Duke University Commonwealth-Studies Center, *The American Economic Impact on Canada* (Durham, N. C., 1959); Joseph Barber, *Good Fences Make Good Neighbors: Why the United States Provokes Canadians* (Indianapolis and New York, 1958); and Brecher and Riesman, *Canada-United States Economic Relations.*

12. Hugh G. J. Aitken, "Defensive Expansionism: The State and Economic Growth in Canada," in Social Science Research Council, *The State and Economic Growth* (New York, 1959), pp. 79–114; see also W. T. Easterbrook and Hugh G. J. Aitken, *Canadian Economic History,* chaps. XVI and XVII, pp. 350–408.

13. Easterbrook and Aitken, *Canadian Economic History,* pp. 372–375.

14. Vernon C. Fowke, "The National Policy — Old and New," *Canadian Journal of Economics and Political Science,* vol. 18, no. 3 (August 1952), pp. 271–286.

15. Long-distance pipelines for oil and natural gas are similar to the railroad in the opportunities they present for national transportation policy. In the case of natural gas, the Canadian government insisted that Ontario and Quebec be served with gas from Alberta before exports to the United States could be permitted, and that the pipeline had to follow an all-Canadian route — a clear case of deliberate reinforcement of the east-west axis. Policy in the case of crude oil has followed different lines, principally because of the availability of low-cost imported crude oil in the Montreal market.

16. R. G. Robertson, "The Material Prospects of the North," *Queen's Quarterly,* vol. LXVI, no. 4 (Winter 1960), pp. 510–518. See also, in this connection, the articles in Frank H. Underhill (ed.), *The Canadian Northwest: Its Potentialities* (Toronto, 1959).

17. Regulations issued by the Canadian government in April, 1960, required that at least 50 per cent of the issued stock of companies obtaining oil and gas leases in the Northwest Territories must be owned by Canadians, or alternatively that the shares of such companies must be listed on a recognized Canadian stock exchange. The significance of these requirements (which do not apply to exploration permits) lies in the fact that a United States subsidiary that incorporates in Canada and lists its stock on Canadian exchanges may lose its right to the very

liberal depletion allowances that it would otherwise enjoy under United States law. Canadian companies have long been at a relative disadvantage in this respect. Their depletion allowances are smaller and are not deductible until all expenditures on exploration and development have first been deducted from gross income (instead of as soon as there is any production from a property, as in the United States). United States subsidiaries, in contrast, may deduct their depletion allowances from gross profits and furthermore are permitted to offset their exploration and development expenditures in Canada against the total income of their parents, including income from refining and marketing. For further discussion, see J. Grant Glassco, *Certain Aspects of Taxation Relating to Investment in Canada by Non-Residents* (Ottawa, 1956), pp. 28–38, and Royal Commission on Canada's Economic Prospects, *Final Report* (Ottawa, 1957), appendix H, pp. 494–497.

18. For an analysis of the emotional and nationalistic appeal of northern development, see J. Howard Richards, "Northland or Promised Land?" *Queen's Quarterly*, vol. LXVI, no. 4 (Winter 1960), pp. 538–547. It is interesting to note that northern development has introduced into Canadian politics the concept of "manifest destiny" once so characteristic of United States expansionism. Mr. Alvin Hamilton, for example, Minister of Northern Affairs and National Resources in the Conservative Cabinet, spoke in the House of Commons of "giving this country dominion . . . from the southern boundary to the Arctic Ocean . . . we feel that it is our destiny manifest by geography [to do so]. If we lose this vision the nation will perish." (Quoted *ibid.*, p. 542.)

19. Frank H. Underhill, "Canadian and American Ties with Europe," *Queen's Quarterly*, vol. LXVI, no. 3 (Autumn 1959), pp. 366–376, at p. 376. See also Underhill, "A Country in Search of an Image," *Saturday Review*, October 24, 1959, pp. 14–16.

CHAPTER V. *Continental Integration and National Identity*

1. See Richard E. Caves, "Europe's Unification and Canada's Trade," *Canadian Journal of Economics and Political Science*, vol. 25, no. 3 (August 1959), pp. 249–258.

2. Dr. Hugh L. Keenleyside, for example, Chairman of the British Columbia Power Commission, has recently proposed that Canada and the United States should work out a system of "selective free trade," the selection being based on the willingness of United States companies to allocate an appropriate portion of their total production to factories established in Canada. This is regarded as being particularly practicable in the case of industries in which monopoly conditions exist, or in which the whole field is covered by a small number of firms. The appearance of discrimination would be avoided by making the same offer of selective free trade to any other country that would similarly

agree to give a fair proportion of its market in specified items to factories established in Canada. See *The Financial Post*, May 7, 1960, p. 25.

3. Section 8 of the Trade Agreements Extension Act of 1958.

4. Commodities involved up to the time of writing have been dental burrs, wool knit gloves, surplus military rifles, semiconductors, cobalt, hydraulic turbines, fluorspar, cordage, wool textiles, watches, analytical balances, wooden boats, thermometers, fine mesh wire cloth, and wool felt. In two cases, photographic shutters and stencil ink, applications for protection were withdrawn.

5. Exports of crude oil and petroleum products from Mexico to the United States have been of minor importance. For all practical purposes, the exemption was given to Canada alone.

6. Executive Office of the President, Office of Civil and Defense Mobilization, *Memorandum of Decision in the Matter of the Petition of American Fluorspar Producers Association* (September 25, 1959).

7. OCDM, *Memorandum of Decision in the Matter of the Petition of the Howe Sound Company* (October 2, 1959).

8. Such a preferential trading area would, of course, be in violation of prior commitments under the General Agreement on Tariffs and Trade.

9. Jacob Viner, *Canada and Its Giant Neighbour*, Alan B. Plaunt Memorial Lectures, Carleton University (Ottawa, 1958), especially pp. 17–21.

APPENDIX

1. Dominion Bureau of Statistics, *Canadian Balance, 1958*, p. 26. p. 26.

2. Samuel Pizer and Frederick Cutler, "U.S. Industry Expands Productive Capacity of Foreign Countries," *Survey of Current Business*, vol. 39, no. 1 (January 1959), pp. 20–24; Pizer and Cutler, "U.S. Industry Expands Investment Abroad," *ibid.*, vol. 39, no. 10 (October 1959), pp. 16–20.

3. If funds received from the parent company in the United States were regarded as "internal," the percentages would be much higher, probably about 75 per cent.

4. D.B.S., *Canadian Balance, 1957*, p. 30.

5. The proportion is probably unusually high because of the substantial disinvestment in inventories that occurred during the 1958 recession.

6. Not all these expenditures, of course, can be classified as "investment" in the sense in which that term is normally used in national-income accounting. Some fraction of the total was undoubtedly devoted to the purchase of assets that already existed rather than the provision of new ones.

Index